New Voices on Early Medieval Sculpture in Britain and Ireland

Edited by

Michael F. Reed

BAR British Series 542
2011

Published in 2016 by
BAR Publishing, Oxford

BAR British Series 542

New Voices on Early Medieval Sculpture in Britain and Ireland

ISBN 978 1 4073 0840 1

© The editor and contributors severally and the Publisher 2011

The Authors' moral rights under the 1988 UK Copyright,
Designs and Patents Act are hereby expressly asserted.

All rights reserved. No part of this work may be copied, reproduced, stored,
sold, distributed, scanned, saved in any form of digital format or transmitted
in any form digitally, without the written permission of the Publisher.

BAR Publishing is the trading name of British Archaeological Reports (Oxford) Ltd.
British Archaeological Reports was first incorporated in 1974 to publish the BAR
Series, International and British. In 1992 Hadrian Books Ltd became part of the BAR
group. This volume was originally published by Archaeopress in conjunction with
British Archaeological Reports (Oxford) Ltd/Hadrian Books Ltd, the Series principal
publisher, in 2011. This present volume is published by BAR Publishing, 2016.

Printed in England

BAR titles are available from:

        BAR Publishing
        122 Banbury Rd, Oxford, OX2 7BP, UK
EMAIL info@barpublishing.com
PHONE +44 (0)1865 310431
FAX   +44 (0)1865 316916
        www.barpublishing.com

Contents

List of contributors..ii
Editor's foreword..iii

Approaching pre-Conquest stone sculpture: historiography and theory..1
Michael F. Reed

Another perspective on the origins and symbolic interpretations of animals in Early Medieval sculpture in Northern England and French Burgundy.. 13
Nicole M. Kleinsmith

Putting memory in its place: sculpture, cemetery topography and commemoration............................32
Zoë L. Devlin

A cross-head from St Mary Castlegate, York, and its affiliations... 42
Victoria Whitworth

Commemoration at York: the significance of Minster 42, 'Costaun's' grave-cover...48
Heather Rawlin-Cushing

Aspects of the Anglo-Saxon tradition in architectural sculpture and articulation: the 'overlap' and beyond.. 57
Malcolm Thurlby

Laser scanning of the inscribed Hiberno-Romanesque arch at Monaincha, Co. Tipperary, Ireland....................... 70
Orla Murphy

List of Contributors

Zoë L. Devlin, Ph.D.
University of York

Nicole M. Kleinsmith, Ph.D.
Independent Scholar, Santa Barbara, California

Orla Murphy, Ph.D.
University College, Cork

Heather Rawlin-Cushing, Ph.D.
Independent Scholar, Suffolk

Michael F. Reed, Ph.D.
York University, Toronto

Prof. Malcolm Thurlby
York University, Toronto

Victoria Whitworth, Ph.D.
Independent Scholar, Orkney

Editor's Foreword

The genesis of this volume was a conference I co-organized at the University of York, U.K., in 2007 entitled "New Voices on Early Medieval Sculpture", generously funded by York's Centre for Medieval Studies and its Sculpture Research School. Many leading academics attended this meeting, resulting in lively (at times heated) exchanges concerning what might be simplistically termed "old" and "new" ideas. Nonetheless, opinions voiced at this conference demonstrated quite clearly that the study of early medieval sculpture in Britain and Ireland is changing. New technologies and evidence (including that which contextualizes sculptural production and patronage), coupled with increased methodological awareness, is generating compelling new interpretations of the role(s) of public art in memorial contexts. Such research emphasizes the significance of patronage and tenurial networks; religious and intellectual movements; and individual and collective identities. Through commitment to interdisciplinary research, the "New Voices" in this volume have interrogated stone sculptures as manifestations of culture, avoiding the artifactual approach which has (far too often) decontextualized objects, minimizing their cultural references. In so doing, they have transcended the methodological restrictions of single-discipline investigation, producing studies that inform literary, historical and sociological research. Ostensibly, these papers demonstrate that traditional approaches to the study of early medieval sculpture (i.e., archaeological and/or art-historical) are obsolete; if our goal is to elucidate the regional and temporal associations of function(s) and meaning(s) as they pertain to stone monuments, then interdisciplinary methodologies, incorporating diverse evidential categories, are required.

I extend sincere thanks to those who contributed to this volume. I hope your scholarship will inspire others to question, debate and explore—as it has me. I am also grateful to the Social Sciences and Humanities Research Council of Canada, whose award of a Postdoctoral Fellowship and a Faculty Small Project Grant (through York University, Toronto) has assisted in completion of this project.

Michael F. Reed, Ph.D.
Social Sciences and Humanities Research Council of Canada Postdoctoral Fellow
York University, Toronto
Feb., 2011.

Approaching pre-Conquest Stone Sculpture:
Historiography and Theory

Michael F. Reed, Ph.D.
York University, Toronto

Historiography

The first substantive discussions of England's pre-Conquest sculpture were products of the antiquarianism associated with nineteenth-century church restoration campaigns and their resultant discoveries of medieval sculpture. Written primarily by churchmen, this corpus laid the foundation for modern pre-Conquest sculptural studies *vis à vis* style, chronology and distribution.[1]

Of nineteenth-century scholars of early English sculpture, William Collingwood was the most influential and certainly the most prolific.[2] Among his earliest work is a series of articles in the *Yorkshire Archaeological Journal* (1907, 1909, 1911 and 1916), in which he develops a descriptive and typological methodology, emphasizing collection, transcription and categorization of data (Collingwood 1907, 267-413, passim; idem 1909, 149-213, passim; idem 1911, 254-302, passim; and idem 1916, 129-299, passim). In fact, in his first paper, "Anglian and Anglo-Danish Sculpture in the North Riding of Yorkshire", he states that "an attempt has been made to collect all accessible remains" (Collingwood 1907, 267). His study is thus similar in both form and organization to J. Romilly Allen's and Joseph Anderson's *The Early Christian Monuments of Scotland* (1903).[3]

Each begins with a lengthy introductory essay discussing materials, techniques, monument types, inscriptions and decoration (including relationships with other media). Subdivisions of each topic are made, with resultant categories defined and explained.[4] A detailed catalogue, augmented by fine line-drawings, accompanies each essay recording the regions' extant pre-Conquest sculpture. Even in this early period, scholars seemingly recognized that precise dating of sculpted stone monuments was exceedingly difficult.[5] Collingwood, Allen and Anderson, for example, date sculpture by century, akin to contemporary researchers who concede that exact dating is impossible in most circumstances.[6]

Collingwood's "Anglian and Anglo-Danish Sculpture at York" (1909) employs the formal typology and organizational strategy introduced in his 1907 paper. This study is an illustrated catalogue of a collection of twenty-five pre-Conquest sculptures preserved in the museum of the York Philosophical Society. Like his treatment of the North Riding material, Collingwood's approach to the Philosophical Society sculptures is primarily descriptive and typological. Though he does not present the collection as a case-study, he does employ some examples to illustrate his chronology of Anglo-Danish sculpture, which he describes as follows (referencing decoration):

> Throughout Northumbria there are sculptures which may be roughly described as presenting Anglian motives with Scandinavian treatment. The first transition (B1) would naturally show Danish motives with Anglian treatment; for local carvers, bred in Anglian traditions, must have been employed by the newcomers to express Danish ideas of ornament and symbolism. In the tenth century, the Anglo-Danes seem to have carved their own stones, having learnt the craft; and throughout stages B2

---

[1] The earliest extant accounts of England's pre-Conquest sculpture are associated with the twelfth century. For example, as evidence of their respective foundations' lengthy histories, William of Malmesbury (d. *ca* 1143) and Symeon of Durham (d. post-1129) describe in relative detail the sculptures at Glastonbury (So) and Durham (Du). The Tudor antiquaries Camden and Leland reference the pre-Conquest sculpture at Reculver (K), Dewsbury (YW) and Bewcastle (Cl). During the Commonwealth period, William Dugdale described and sketched the tenth-century sculpture at Penrith (Cl); and other late seventeenth- and eighteenth-century travellers also discussed England's pre-Conquest sculpture in some detail. Such early accounts are usually anecdotal, however, only occasionally preserving oblique references to sculptures' location, shape, size and decorative features. See Arnold (I, 1882-1885, 38); Stubbs (I, 1887, 25); Toulmin-Smith (IV, 1909, 59-61); Camden (1588; 1607, 565, 644); and Bailey (1980, 27).

[2] Collingwood's scholarship was esteemed by his contemporaries. For example, referencing the pre-Conquest sculpture of northern England, particularly free-standing crosses, Johannes Bröndsted states that Collingwood has "provided a nearly complete Corpus, arranged and treated chronologically, the only systematic work in English archaeology dealing with these domains and of the utmost importance for any study of this material" (Bröndsted 1924, 14). Jane Hawkes has recently discussed Collingwood's scholarship emphasizing its methodological and theoretical implications. See Hawkes (2007, 142-152, passim).

[3] Collingwood acknowledges Allen's assistance in the preparation of his paper: "Mr. J. Romilly Allen F.S.A., Hon. F.S.A. Scot., has most kindly read the proof of this paper, and supplied four sites previously overlooked, together with valuable remarks which are acknowledged in the text" (Collingwood 1907, 267).

[4] Collingwood's typology of cross-heads (differentiating, principally, between free-arms and wheel-heads and signified by alphabetic identifiers) seemingly influenced Rosemary Cramp as a model for her formal and decorative typology of Anglo-Saxon sculpture. See Collingwood (1907, 272-274); and Cramp (1984; 1991, passim).

[5] In fact, Collingwood states: "We have really very few fixed dates to rest upon" (Collingwood 1907, 294).

[6] See, for example, Bailey (1980, 45-75, esp. 73-75); and Cramp (1984; 1991, xlvii-xlviii).

and B3 they carried out their own ideas, tinged first with Irish and then with Midland character (Collingwood 1909, 152).

This linear evolutionary model is somewhat modified in Collingwood's "Anglian and Anglo-Danish Sculpture in the East Riding, with addenda relating to the North Riding" (1911). In this study, Collingwood discusses twenty-four examples in his characteristic essay/catalogue format. However, he adds "transitional forms" to his linear model such as "AC (Anglian revival, or Anglian tradition and late execution, without Scandinavian character) and BC (Danish survival in eleventh century technique)" (Collingwood 1911, 255). This is a significant development in the study of England's pre-Conquest sculpture; at an early stage, there is acknowledgement that methodology must be flexible and responsive to extant evidence.

Collingwood's "Anglian and Anglo-Danish sculpture in the West Riding, with addenda to the North and East Ridings and York, and a general review of the Early Christian monuments of Yorkshire" (1916) builds on his earlier publications in the *Yorkshire Archaeological Journal* and attempts to redress the absence of a national catalogue of pre-Conquest English sculpture akin to Allen's and Anderson's *Early Christian Monuments of Scotland*. Presented in his characteristic format, this work is monumental in scale; it records all extant examples, illustrating most, and presents exceptionally detailed categorizations, discussions and indices of decorative elements, sculptural forms, inscriptions and techniques (Collingwood 1916, 261-299).[7] Like Collingwood's earlier *Yorkshire Archaeological Journal* articles, his approach is primarily descriptive and typological.

Collingwood's methodology evolves in the work for which he is best known: *Northumbrian Crosses of the Pre-Norman Age* (1927). Like "Anglian and Anglo-Danish sculpture in the West Riding ... ", this study can also be interpreted as a *naissant* metanarrative of England's pre-Conquest sculptural traditions, approaching the national scope of the *Early Christian Monuments of Scotland*. Unlike his earlier studies, however, *Northumbrian Crosses* advocates a processual approach, emphasizing chronology. For example, Collingwood states that:

> This book is ... an attempt to consider ancient styles as phases of a process, and to place the examples in series. Monographs on the more famous monuments are valuable; so are descriptive catalogues. They provide the material for classification. But until the classes are formed, and then connected into some reasonable scheme, we have not done all we can (Collingwood, "Preface", 1927; 1989, n.p.).

Collingwood begins his chronology with what he terms the "rude stone pillar" (Early Christian cross-marked stones) and then traces the development of Anglo-Saxon sculpture from roods to free-standing crosses. A chronology of Anglo-Scandinavian sculpture follows,[8] emphasizing the two forms most closely associated with Scandinavian colonists: the wheel-head cross and the hogback.

The final chapter of the book, "Outcomes of Northumbrian Monumental Art", is perhaps its most significant. It succinctly presents evidence for archaism in some later pre-Conquest sculpture, including architectural decoration at Monkwearmouth (Su) (Collingwood 1927; 1989, 174-184). This argument is indicative of an evolution in Collingwood's work (and, by association, in early sculptural studies generally). A substantive progression is discernible from the descriptive/typological approach popularized by Allen and Anderson to one in which contextualization and interpretation play increasingly important roles.

This evolution in early sculptural studies is most apparent in *Anglo-Saxon Sculpture* (1937), the final instalment of Gerard Baldwin Brown's multi-volume *The Arts in Early England* (1903, 1915, 1921, 1930, 1937). Though Baldwin Brown discusses select Anglo-Saxon stone sculptures (including the iconic Northumbrian Ruthwell and Bewcastle crosses) in an earlier volume (Baldwin Brown 1921, 58-305), his polemics on methodology are reserved for *Anglo-Saxon Sculpture*.

Throughout this volume, he evokes the theory popularized by Johannes Bröndsted that the Hellenistic character of *ca* eighth- and early ninth-century carvings (including the Ruthwell, Df, Bewcastle, Cl, Easby, YN, and Reculver, K, crosses) is demonstrative of eastern artistic training, implying that foreign sculptors (identified as "Syrian") were active in the north and south of England in the Middle Saxon period (Bröndsted 1924, 16-37, esp. 37, 88; Baldwin Brown 1937, 116-133, 185). He also opines that England's extant, pre-Conquest stone crosses should be interpreted as objects of singular artistic achievement, demonstrating advanced individual creativity, rather than manifestations of formulaic craft (for example, Baldwin Brown 1937, 250-253).

Though such vestiges of connoisseurship are apparent in *Anglo-Saxon Sculpture*, Baldwin Brown (like Collingwood) contextualizes and interprets stone monuments; however, his analysis (albeit speculative) also explores, in relative depth, the social history of pre-Conquest sculpture, including manufacture and use(s) (ibid., 93-115, 165-183, 212-226, 248-268). In this regard, *Anglo-Saxon Sculpture* is informed by William

---

[7] This information is presented in an addendum entitled, "General Review of the Early Christian Monuments of Yorkshire". Collingwood employs Allen's typology of interlace patterns; and in form and content, this addendum closely resembles Cramp's *Grammar of Anglo-Saxon Ornament*. See n. 4.

[8] Collingwood employs two descriptors for Anglo-Scandinavian colonists in England: "Anglo-Danish" (inhabitants of Yorkshire) and "Anglo-Norse" (inhabitants of Cumbria).

Stevens' *The Cross in the Life and Literature of the Anglo-Saxons* (1904), the first history of the cross in Anglo-Saxon society.

Acknowledging his interest in social history, Baldwin Brown is critical of Collingwood's *Northumbrian Crosses*. He notes that much of Collingwood's data on "material and technique", which had been included in his numerous *Yorkshire Archaeological Journal* articles (see above, 1-3), is "omitted to incorporate" (Baldwin Brown 1937, 135). Furthermore, he observes that:

> Important archaeological facts or problems which have a direct bearing on questions of date or of provenance are lightly blown aside as if they were not worth attention for more than a moment (ibid., 135).

Baldwin Brown's methodological approach, which attempts to define stone sculptures as manifestations of culture through contextualizing evidence (literary and material) distinguishes *Anglo-Saxon Sculpture* as a seminal work in the early history of pre-Conquest sculptural studies.

This tentative movement toward location of Britain's early medieval sculpture in its socio-political context(s) continued throughout the first half of the twentieth century, albeit with a noticeable hiatus during the Second World War. The vast documentative/typological studies of Allan, Anderson and Collingwood continued to influence scholars including Victor Nash-Williams and Françoise Henry. Nash-Williams' *The Early Christian Monuments of Wales* (1950) and much of Henry's work, including *Irish Art in the Early Christian Period* (1940) and *Irish High Crosses* (1964), replicate the national scope of earlier research, yet, like Baldwin Brown, develop methodologies of contextualization and interpretation more fully than Collingwood.[9]

By the 1970s, the study of Insular sculpture was well-developed within the growing field of Medieval Studies,[10] and several scholars (Rosemary Cramp, Richard Bailey and James Lang) displayed particular interest in Anglo-Scandinavian material. Building upon Collingwood's work, they undertook important projects which, collectively, brought attention, interest and significance to the corpus of Anglo-Scandinavian sculpture.

Replicating the sequence of English sculptural studies, early work in this specialization was largely descriptive and typological. Like Collingwood's initial preoccupation with formal typologies (thereby distinguishing Anglian and Scandinavian material), scholars in the 1970s were primarily concerned with issues of date and frequently employed iconographic and formalist analyses of the carving as chronological tools.[11] For example, in his 1973 article, Lang argues that the figural scene (which had previously been interpreted as a pagan burial) on a cross from Ryedale (YN), known as "Middleton 2", is a portrait of an enthroned man surrounded by symbols of his secular authority. In addition, he argues that peculiarities in the execution of the beast panel on "Middleton 2" are developments or misunderstandings of other Jellinge-style animals at Ryedale. Thus, Lang interprets idiosyncrasies in the style of "Middleton 2" as a modified continuation or final example of the Jellinge style in England rather than its unsteady beginning. This later context for "Middleton 2" is supported by Lang's rejection of the "pagan burial" interpretation of the figural scene (Lang 1973, 16-25, passim).

In "The Chronology of Viking-Age Sculpture in Northumbria" (1978), Bailey also addresses the issue of Anglo-Scandinavian sculpture and the attribution of date. He begins by noting the many problems associated with this task including the sheer size of the corpus, its reliance on a limited repertoire of dated motifs, the paucity of securely-dated examples and the possibility that incompetence can explain idiosyncratic carving (Bailey 1978, 173-203, at 175). Bailey then offers three guidelines for the ascription of date to Northumbria's Anglo-Scandinavian sculpture. He begins by referencing textual evidence, the Durham *Historia de Sancto Cuthberto* (*ca* tenth or eleventh century), which implies that Cumbria was unaffected by Viking raids or settlement until the second decade of the tenth century. Coupled with evidence of Cumbrian elites with Anglian names as late as *ca* 915 and Lindisfarne monks seeking refuge in Cumbria from Viking raids in the late ninth century, Bailey proposes that sculpture associated with Scandinavian patrons cannot predate the first or second decade of the tenth century in western Northumbria (ibid., 177). Secondly, he refers to Collingwood's arguments expressed in the *Yorkshire Archaeological Journal* which associate the wheel-head cross in Northumbria with Viking settlement. He summarizes what is known of this sculptural form as follows:

> a) It does *not* occur in England with ornament which is clearly pre-Viking.
> b) It does occur in England both with animal, figural and knotwork ornament which derives from Scandinavia and with patterns which are frequently associated with those Scandinavian-derived motifs.
> c) In Ireland and in western Scotland, notably at Iona, the ring-head occurs in a free-cut (non-slab) form at a date before the Viking invasions (ibid., 178).

---

[9] See Nash-Williams (1950, 1-5); Henry (1940; 1965, 1-10); and idem (1964, 1-4).

[10] The label "Medieval Studies" is used cautiously with reference to the 1970s. The formation of Medieval Studies departments is generally associated with the late 1970s to mid-1980s. Earlier medieval research was generally conducted in those departments which would become the "parents" of Medieval Studies (including languages, History and Archaeology). With reference to Anglo-Scandinavian sculptural studies in the early 1970s, most research was undertaken by archaeologists.

[11] "Iconographic" analyses employ semiotic decoding of both figural and non-figural ornament, whereas "formalist" study utilizes typological evidence.

Viking settlement in Northumbria is securely dated to the tenth century and was the result of eastward movement from Ireland to England. Therefore, Bailey emphasizes that wheel-heads in Northumbria cannot predate the tenth century. Finally, he offers evidence that templates were used in the carving of Cumbrian monuments. He notes that template-analysis permits identification of contemporary work; thus, together with traditional stylistic inquiry, sculptures can be distinguished which belong, roughly, to the same generation (ibid., 185). In summary, Bailey argues that historical, formal and stylistic evidence suggests that Anglo-Scandinavian sculpture in Northumbria does not pre-date the tenth century.

Such chronological study of Anglo-Scandinavian sculpture has been facilitated by developments in formalist analysis. In the 1970s, scholars initiated reinterpretation of the material, documenting its apparent responsiveness to cultural stimuli. Cramp briefly discusses relationships between early Anglo-Scandinavian and Mercian sculpture in "Schools of Mercian Sculpture" (Cramp 1977, 191-233, at 218, 224-225), while other scholars presented detailed case studies of the evidence, examining its apparent role(s) in the construction of identities. For example, in "Continuity and Innovation in Anglo-Scandinavian Sculpture: A Study of the Metropolitan School at York" (1978), Lang demonstrates that the emergence of Anglo-Scandinavian styles was characterized by continuous transition, that residual Anglian conservatism continued through the tenth century, even in areas of Scandinavian settlement, and that many elements associated with Scandinavian styles have Insular origins (Lang 1978, 145-172, at 145). These conclusions are based on an examination of the funerary sculpture excavated from beneath York Minster by Derek Phillips in 1971. Lang posits that these monuments are crucial to an understanding of Anglo-Scandinavian sculptural practices throughout Yorkshire:

> They represent the art of a metropolitan centre where political, ecclesiastical and commercial influences had their focus. The sculptors of the trading city of York were more likely to have been receptive to outside fashionable trends, have enjoyed more prosperous and accomplished workshops and have been in a position to affect the local provincial art within a radius of the capital (ibid., 145-146).

Through this case study of the Metropolitan School, Lang determines that English, perhaps even Mercian, exemplars were the principal influence on the sculptors of York; and though Scandinavian design elements are overt amongst the school's extant work, they do not obfuscate the monuments' underlying Anglian traditions (ibid., 153).

Scholarly interest in the carved programmes of Anglo-Scandinavian sculpture continued through the 1980s, culminating with Bailey's *Viking Age Sculpture in Northern England*. However, unlike the descriptive/typological approaches of earlier periods, this work is arranged thematically. Bailey begins his study with historical contextualization and then progresses to a discussion of chronology. The factors which facilitate attributions of date (find-context, inscription and style) are assessed in detail; although Bailey concludes that in most instances it is not possible to date a monument more precisely than "Viking-period" (Bailey 1980, 74).[12] Following his discussion of chronology, Bailey assesses the English inheritance in Anglo-Scandinavian sculpture and the form, decoration, date and possible function of hogback monuments.

In his subsequent chapter, "Gods Heroes and Christians", Bailey interprets the pagan iconography characteristic of many Anglo-Scandinavian monuments. He notes how in the nineteenth century, a rediscovery of England's Germanic past awoke general interest in pre-Christian religion. This societal trend influenced other scholars; and, with reference to the iconography of Anglo-Scandinavian sculpture, pre-Christian scenes were interpreted as irrefutable evidence of pagan practice. In fact, Romilly Allen had stated that "it is in the highest degree unlikely that heathen legends were ever adapted to Christian purposes" (Allen, quoted in Bailey 1980, 101). However, following the *naissance* of specialist studies in the 1970s, the iconography of Anglo-Scandinavian sculpture was theorized and interpreted in new ways. Bailey summarizes how Wayland and Sigurd scenes, together with the iconographic programme of the Gosforth Cross ("Gosforth 1"), can be interpreted as Christian paradigms (Bailey 1980, 101-142). He also suggests that the evocation of religious ambiguity by select scenes may have been deliberate (ibid., 142).

Of Bailey's remaining chapters, "Sculpture and History: a Wider Perspective" and "The Sculptor at Work" are particularly important. The former acknowledges the potential richness of interdisciplinary research and suggests place-names and settlement evidence could help demystify the Middleton Cross ("Middleton 2"; ibid., 209-213); whereas the latter discusses aspects of the carving process, including preparation of the stone, templates and carving techniques. Prior to publication of *Viking Age Sculpture*, the technical processes involved in sculptural production were noticeably understudied, albeit with the notable exceptions of Collingwood's *Yorkshire Archaeological Journal* articles and Baldwin Brown's *Anglo-Saxon Sculpture*.

Though *Viking Age Sculpture* is region-specific, it does not discuss its subject in isolation; the sculpture is placed in its historical context, its methods of production are assessed, and most other related issues (including decoration, function and patronage) are considered in varying degrees. This broad approach constitutes a marked evolution in methodology; *ca* 1980,

---

[12] The role of templates in attributions of date is also discussed (ibid., 242-254).

acknowledgement that contextualization and interpretation are fundamental components of sculptural research is seemingly evident.

While *Viking Age Sculpture in Northern England* has facilitated interpretation of sculptural production in Late Saxon northern England, the *Corpus of Anglo-Saxon Stone Sculpture* (1984-), presently in eight volumes under the general editorship of Rosemary Cramp (Cramp 1984; Bailey and Cramp 1988; Lang, et al. 1991; Tweddle, et al. 1995; Everson and Stocker 1999; Lang 2002; Cramp 2006; Coatsworth 2008), is redressing the void observed by Collingwood over eighty years ago: the absence of a national record of English pre-Conquest sculpture akin to *The Early Christian Monuments of Scotland* (Collingwood, "Preface", 1927; 1989, n.p.). Each volume of the *Corpus* is preceded by Cramp's "General Introduction to the *Corpus of Anglo-Saxon Stone Sculpture*", functioning as a handbook of Anglo-Saxon and Anglo-Scandinavian sculptural ornament, codifying the typologies and terminology associated with their study. Each volume of the *Corpus* is an illustrated catalogue preceded by introductory essays addressing various topics including stone types, carving techniques, style and chronology. The methodology employed by the various authors of the *Corpus* volumes utilizes both typological and interpretive approaches. This unification of what might be termed "historic" and "contemporary" methodologies *vis à vis* pre-Conquest English sculpture is attributable to the *Corpus*' function: provision of basic data for each extant sculpture (location, size, material, decoration) and contextualization of sculptural production and use in specific regions. Through evocation of the metanarratives characteristic of the early to mid-twentieth century, the *Corpus* is also demonstrative of the apparent cyclical nature of early English sculptural studies.

Since publication of *Viking Age Sculpture* and the various volumes of the *Corpus of Anglo-Saxon Stone Sculpture*, interdisciplinary research has become increasingly important to the interpretation and contextualization of Anglo-Scandinavian sculpture. Place-names evidence, settlement archaeology and the history of lordship have each contributed to an understanding of the distribution, decoration and patronage of sculpture in pre-Conquest England. Interdisciplinary publications such as *Cultures in Contact: Scandinavian Settlement in England in the Ninth and Tenth Centuries* (2000) identify the socio-political context(s) in which sculpture was commissioned, produced and displayed (Hadley and Richards, eds., 2000a, passim), without which any attempt to reconstruct sculptures' uses, meanings and functions would be impossible.

In conclusion, contemporary pre-Conquest sculptural studies are the product of nineteenth- and early twentieth-century interest in Britain's extant stone-working legacy. Early researchers employed descriptive and typological methodologies in compiling full surveys of early English sculpture, often approaching national scale. With the advent of specialist research in Anglo-Scandinavian sculpture in the 1970s, agendas prioritized decorative and iconographic interpretation, culminating in the publication of Bailey's *Viking Age Sculpture in Northern England* (1980). The sculptural legacy of the Anglo-Scandinavians was then portrayed as a distinct cultural artifact rather than a debased Anglo-Saxon form. Recently, sculptural studies have benefited from the interdisciplinary research promoted by Bailey, with other evidential categories contributing to an understanding of patronage, distribution and function(s). With the *Corpus of Anglo-Saxon Stone Sculpture* nearing completion, this expanding inquiry will merge with the descriptive and typological methodologies popularized by early researchers; in so doing, the definitive corpus that Collingwood sought will be realized.

Sculpture and Archaeological Theory

The "national" surveys of Insular sculpture published throughout the early to mid-twentieth century emphasize sculpture's intrinsic importance rather than its evidence of cultural processes (Allen and Anderson 1903; 1993, passim; Collingwood 1927; 1989, passim; Nash-Williams 1950, passim; and Henry 1964, passim). However, since the 1960s (especially post-1980), various theoretical and methodological strategies have been applied to its study, perhaps reflecting the general "theorization" of archaeology in the latter twentieth century, illustrated by the abundance of theory courses in university curricula, by the volume of scholarship devoted to theory since 1960, and by the advent of archaeological colloquia devoted exclusively to theoretical issues. Within this culture of theory, the current traditions of archaeological thought (*processual*—social evolution, taphonomy and middle-range theory, and *post-processual*—hermeneutics, structuration theory and political commitment; Johnson 1999; 2000, 116), including instances when they seemingly converge, can potentially enrich the study of pre-Conquest sculpture, though their limitations must be acknowledged.

Though Anglo-Scandinavian sculpture is first theorized as a distinct cultural artifact in Bailey's *Viking Age Sculpture*, and strong currents of archaeological thought are implicit throughout the text, this study is not explicitly theoretical.[13] Rather, it is essentially an exercise

---

[13] In their "Editors' Foreword" to the Collins Archaeology series (of which *Viking Age Sculpture* is the first volume), Cherry Lavell and Eric Wood state: "This series is intended for the reader who wishes to know what is happening in a given field. He may not be a trained archaeologist, although he may be attending courses in some aspect of the subject; he may want to know more about his locality, or about some particular aspect, problem or technique; or he may be merely generally interested in the roots of our civilization, and how knowledge about them is obtained ... The series presents books of moderate length, well illustrated, on various aspects of archaeology ... They are written in straightforward language by experts ... [and] ... are essentially up-to-date and down-to-earth". Clearly, the series' editors assume that Bailey's audience will not be a specialist one; therefore, with reference to language, arguments and general presentation, the book appeals to a broad audience. See Lavell and Wood, "Editors' Foreword" in Bailey (1980, v-vi, at v-vi).

in what can be termed middle-range theory. From his observation of the static archaeological record (extant Anglo-Scandinavian sculpture), Bailey forms theories about the Danelaw. These contextualize his data, situating them within the socio-political environment of tenth-century eastern England. Without these linking or "contextualizing" theories, Bailey's data would have no relationship to the historical Danelaw.[14]

An explicit example of middle-range theory in *Viking Age Sculpture* is the discussion of sculptural templates:

> Mechanical aids were employed. We can trace their use most easily if we look at the cross-heads; and, as an example, I take a group of heads which are now in the Tees valley churches of Brompton *YN*, Northallerton *YN* and Kirklevington *CL* ... It is possible to show that at least ten of the crosses in these churches were carved by using the same template curve (Bailey 1980, 240).

Lewis Binford noted that independent sources of information (such as texts or, in this instance, sculptural templates) could be used to build "robust" arguments (quoted in Johnson 1999; 2000, 155; see also 48-63), akin to Erwin Panofsky's theorization of iconology in art historical circles. Such information functions as "pre-existing" middle-range theories, often contemporaneous with the data it contextualizes. Thus, it is valued for its perceived accuracy, drawn from temporal proximity to evidence.

Bailey's treatment of data in *Viking Age Sculpture* is evocative of the post-processualist movement (similar in many respects to post-modernism). For middle-range theorists, data are atheoretical. Bailey, however, theorizes much of the data employed in *Viking Age Sculpture*. For example, he assumes that traces of paint on some extant Anglo-Scandinavian sculptures is evidence that "many, if not most" were painted (Bailey 1980, 25). He then offers a series of assumptions about the effect of painting monuments, both upon the viewer and upon the monuments themselves:

> We are seeing ... [sculpture] at a stage before completion. Any use of gesso would change the contours of a carving; miscuttings would not be visible; changes in geological colouring would be masked. The confusion of lightly-incised lines which decorate carvings ... would be clarified and it would be possible to add details of facial features, clothing, foliage and beasts to the basic carved forms (ibid., 26).

Furthermore, throughout his text, Bailey suggests that the spatial and numerical distribution of Anglo-Scandinavian sculpture is indicative of mass consumption by the Danelaw populace and reflects a uniform density of settlement (ibid., 176-206). Again, data is theorized resulting in the abandonment of its assumed neutrality. However plausible and even likely such theories are, their underlying assumptions require examination.

One of Bailey's more recent works, *England's Earliest Sculptors* (1997), illustrates a development in his theoretical approach. Concerned primarily with chronology, this work surveys England's sculptural legacy from the seventh century to the Norman Conquest. Unlike *Viking Age Sculpture*, however, Bailey explicitly utilizes evidence from other disciplines (including literature and art history) to support his arguments. He also places importance on chronological studies in other media:

> The current approach to sculptural chronology ... draws upon the dating systems that have evolved for the other art forms of manuscript and metalwork. Detailed ... [studies have been undertaken] by David Wilson, Lesley Webster and James Graham-Campbell on metalwork; ... [and the dating] of painted books has been refined by ... Julian and Michelle Brown (Bailey 1997, 17).

Bailey's explicit adoption of evidence and methodology from other disciplines is illustrative of a development in post-processual thought, namely, that divisions between disciplines are arbitrary; and as the post-processualist rejects the notion of metanarratives, evidence from other sources becomes not only valid, but necessary (Johnson 1999; 2000, 162). However, specific forms of inquiry encounter specific sets of variables, and such variables may or may not hinder use of evidence in other contexts.

For example, Bailey states that the current approach to sculptural chronology has drawn upon dating systems from manuscript and metalwork studies. Chronological investigations of these media (especially manuscripts) reveal variables that are not present in sculpted stone. Attributing date to manuscripts may be facilitated by the presence of a colophon; by assessing paleographic and/or linguistic details; and by codicological examination. Therefore, to what extent are specific dating techniques genuinely applicable to all media? Some dating criteria transcend media (for example, style, the presence of inscriptions and associations with specific people and/or events). Media-specific variables, however, are anomalous; even style-analysis is somewhat qualified by regional variation, artistic ability and the characteristics of specific materials. While style-analysis can identify general queues that facilitate dating, region- and medium-specific characteristics qualify its chronological precision.

Together with Richard Bailey's collective scholarship, the *Corpus of Anglo-Saxon Stone Sculpture* is the most authoritative source for the production, decoration and function of Late Saxon sculpture. While each *Corpus* volume is informed by developments in archaeological thought, the theoretical interests of their respective

---

[14] For a summary of middle-range theory, see Johnson (1999; 2000, 49-63).

authors are largely implicit. Nonetheless, the *Corpus* does demonstrate how analyses of static data sets can vary depending on modes of inquiry. Obvious examples are the function(s) of Late Saxon sculpture in the Danelaw and whether its distribution reflects settlement patterns.

In the second *Corpus* volume, Bailey and Cramp interpret Anglo-Scandinavian sculpture using middle-range theory. They emphasize (as Bailey did in 1980) the Christian context for sculptural use (largely for memorialization, perhaps as expressions of faith), interpret iconography in a Christian context and suggest that the size and distribution of the sculptural corpus indicates broad consumption in the Danelaw and reflects a uniform settlement density (Bailey and Cramp 1988, 12-13, 24-40, 100-104). This approach contrasts with Paul Everson's and David Stocker's in the Lincolnshire volume. In their analysis of the county's Anglo-Scandinavian sculpture, they determine that secular agendas played important roles in the erection of stone monuments and that their number and distribution is evidence of social competition between large elite groups (Everson and Stocker 1999, 69-87, esp. 76-79).[15] They suggest that such objects emulate the tastes of incoming mercantile elites from York and Scandinavia (ibid., 80-84). Implicit in Everson's and Stocker's arguments is the notion of conflict between the residents of Lincoln and the incoming merchants. This conflict (specifically, dissimilarity in display of elite status) is associated with Marxist theory and is demonstrated by Everson's and Stocker's presentation of oppositions in both artifact and artifact-placement as evidence of societal relationships.[16] Everson's and Stocker's approach also evokes the concepts of "core" and "periphery", fundamental components of world systems theory (Trigger 1989; 2006, 303-312, 404). In this respect, changes in one locale (migration for example) impact the other.

As the post-processualist school of archaeological thought has developed, interdisciplinary research has increased in both frequency and importance. As mentioned above, place-names evidence, settlement archaeology and the history of lordship have each contributed to the interpretation of the distribution, decoration and patronage of Late Saxon sculpture. Interdisciplinary publications, such as Hadley's and Richards' *Cultures in Contact* (2000a), reconstruct the socio-political context(s) for sculptural production. In their paper, "Introduction: Interdisciplinary Approaches to the Scandinavian Settlement", Hadley and Richards reiterate the importance of interdisciplinary collaboration to Danelaw studies:

Throughout this volume it is apparent that exciting new interpretations of the Scandinavian impact on England are possible on the basis of a re-evaluation of the existing evidence, and by asking new questions. It is also clear that the future requires interdisciplinary collaboration. In exposing new areas for research, it is often reconciling the different interpretations indicated by different categories of evidence that provides the greatest challenges (Hadley and Richards 2000b, 13).

They also stress the necessity of redefining the Danelaw's settlement, characterizing it as a series of regional variations rather than a single, homogeneous assimilation (ibid., 3.). In so doing, Hadley and Richards advocate a functionalist or systems thinking approach for Danelaw inquiry (one which defines a culture as an "intercommunicating network of attributes or entities forming a complex whole"; Clarke, quoted in Johnson 1999; 2000, 67).[17] The strength of this theoretical model is its avoidance of monocausal explanations; however, it fails to examine why particular strategies were favoured in cultural evolution (Johnson 1999; 2000, 77). Thus, Hadley and Richards suggest that Anglo-Scandinavian lordship should be understood in terms of the "administrative, legal, diplomatic and ideological world of early medieval society", rather than as a series of military victories (Hadley and Richards 2000b, 6).

Hadley and Richards also address the notion of Anglo-Scandinavian identity in their introductory essay. They characterize Danelaw ethnicity as a social construction, "malleable and historically situated" and "transmitted and transmuted over time and space" (ibid; and Innes, quoted in Hadley and Richards 2000b, 6). These perceptions are related to post-processual archaeology's belief that culture is adaptive to an external environment and its notion of individual agency (the relationship between people and social rules is characterized by creative manipulation rather than passive adherence).

With the sheer volume of courses, scholarship and colloquia devoted explicitly to thought and process, contemporary archaeology can be characterized as a culture of theory. As such, researchers must familiarize themselves with the schools of thought informing this and related disciplines so they can engage with theorized data in an active and critical way. In so doing, interpretation of specific material culture (for example, Anglo-Saxon sculpture) will be informed by awareness of the assumed factors (both implicit and explicit) affecting its production, appearance and reception and the relationship(s) between those assumptions and methodology.

---

[15] See also Stocker (2000, 200-206).

[16] "A number of important Marxist concepts have been introduced into British and American archaeology as alternatives to the tenets of processual archaeology. Foremost among these is a concern to explain sociocultural change in terms of a general theoretical framework that accords a central role to social relations ... Social conflicts arising from contradictory interests are identified as vital and pervasive features of human societies and a major source of change" (Trigger 1989; 2006, 339-340).

[17] See also Trigger (1989; 2006, 303-312, 404).

Sculpture and Art Historical Theory

Both archaeology and art history interpret objects as cultural artifacts. The former locates them within evidential systems, establishing various shared approximates which, collectively, reflect cultures, groups and/or their beliefs;[18] while through intensive study of individual objects, the latter facilitates contextualization of inconsistencies and incongruities, identifying what Fred Orton terms "historical and cultural specificity" (Orton 1999, 217). Though typological analysis is paradigmatic in Anglo-Saxon sculptural studies (ibid., 220), other forms of inquiry less reliant on typologies (iconographic for example) have contributed to an understanding of the patronage and reception of this corpus; thus, the suitability of art historical methodologies for contextualizing sculptural production and display should be assessed.

Jane Hawkes has observed that style-analysis, which characterizes or influences much of the scholarship devoted to Anglo-Saxon stone-carving, has been recently discredited by both archaeologists and art historians (Hawkes 2007, 142). Through functionalist theories of stylistic inconsistency, this methodology has been challenged by some archaeologists since the 1940s,[19] though Sidebottom suggests that style-analysis is inherently unreliable because it represents an "art historical method".[20] Conversely, this approach is discredited by art historians for its perceived obsolescence; with the notable exceptions of medieval art and architectural history, stylistic inquiry has not dominated art historical scholarship since the 1950s (Hawkes 2007, 142). Nonetheless, stylistic (in)consistency, theorized by Sidebottom as "regional variation" rather than "temporal disparity" is pertinent to pre-Conquest sculpture (Sidebottom 1999, 209);[21] it can inform discussions of patronage and identity, centres of sculptural production and the apparent regional impact of socio-political movements.

As discussed above (p. 1), the *naissance* of Anglo-Saxon sculptural research is associated with the late nineteenth and early twentieth centuries, particularly with Collingwood's work on northern England. Throughout his various studies, culminating in *Northumbrian Crosses*, Collingwood characterizes sculptural development as linear progression, employing style as a chronological measure. Though some post-medieval art historians associate style-analysis with the *connoisseur*, thereby marginalizing the methodology as "un-academic" (Hawkes 2007, 143),[22] the early historiography of Germanic art, including Anglo-Saxon sculpture as specialist study, was influenced by contemporary philosophy; Hawkes associates the resultant analytic use of style with "post-Darwinian, later nineteenth-century constructs of imperial synthesis" (Hawkes 2007, 143), exemplified by John Lubbock's *Prehistoric Times* (1865; 1913).[23] Thus, early stylistic interrogation of Anglo-Saxon sculpture, reflecting the apparent quantifiability of evolutionary systems, is historically informed and situated; its pejorative association with connoisseurship should be reconsidered.

Collingwood's early research on northern England's Anglo-Saxon sculpture is contemporaneous with Montelius' *Der Orient und Europa* (1899), *Die typologische Methode* (1903) and Salin's *Die altgermanische thierornamentik* (1904), archaeological treatises which define style as temporal constructs.[24] This premise is implicit in Collingwood's first study of the Yorkshire material (1907), suggesting both awareness and adoption of contemporary "archaeological" methodology (Collingwood 1907, passim).[25] This stylistic approach, however, contrasts with Collingwood's initial commentaries on Anglo-Saxon sculpture, influenced, particularly, by the tutelage of John Ruskin.

Following his studies at Oxford and London, Collingwood wrote *Philosophy of Ornament* (1883), informed by Ruskin's theories of "Ideal" and "Real" Art. According to Ruskin, the "Ideal" is associated with the Aristotelian concepts of order, symmetry and the essential and is defined as "dead barbarism" (Ruskin, "The two paths", §28-29, 1905, 274-275; Mynor 1994, 33-35; Hawkes 2007, 145); whereas "Real Art" is equated with "living barbarism", whose "every line ... is prophetic of power, and has in it the sure dawn of day", somewhat evocative of Plato's "*techne*" and "*mimesis*" (Ruskin, "The two paths", §30, 1905, 275; Mynor 1994, 31; Hawkes 2007, 145). Furthermore, Ruskin associates "Real Art" with spirituality and learning, interpreting the Anglo-Saxons' artistic legacy as "some likeness of the realities of sacred event in which they had been instructed" (Ruskin, "The pleasures of England", lecture I: "The pleasures of learning", §28-29, 1908, 435-436; Hawkes 2007, 146). Thus, in *The Art Teaching of John Ruskin* (1891), Collingwood interprets Anglo-Saxon material as "Real Art" (Collingwood 1891, 38), with its implied vitality, cognition and literacy. His stylistic

---

[18] See, for example, Trigger (1989; 2006, 1-4).
[19] For example, Walter Taylor's study of asymmetry in Coahuila Cave basketry designs in the southwestern United States. Quoted in Trigger (1989; 2006, 279).
[20] This implies that art historical methods impair archaeology and/or its reputation (Sidebottom 1999, 206). See also Wicker (1999, 161-171, passim).
[21] A similar rejection of style as chronological indicator is advanced by Bertil Almgren. Cf. Almgren (1955, passim); and Wilson (1959, passim).

[22] See also Mynor (1994, 129-137). Morelli's treatise on Italian painters informed and popularized the association between style-analysis and connoisseurship. See Morelli (1892-1893, passim). See also Fernie, ed. (1995, 103-115). As an analytic tool, style was first employed in archaeology by Thomsen in 1836 and popularized in England by Worsaae in 1849. See Thomsen (1836, passim); Worsaae (1849, passim); and idem (1852, passim). See also Trigger (1989; 2006, 73-79). Evans' scholarship on Anglo-Saxon coins also employs style-analysis. See Evans (1850, passim); and Geake (1997, 3-4).
[23] Lubbock (1865; 1913, passim). See also Trigger (1989; 2006, 114-118).
[24] See also Bakka (1958, passim); and Hawkes (2007, 151).
[25] This theory is explicit in his subsequent study of the West Riding sculptures. See Collingwood (1916, 261-299, esp. 291-293).

approach to Anglo-Saxon sculpture is only evident in his various studies of regional groups (published in archaeological journals) suggesting, as Hawkes observes:

> That while the art historian could consider the carvings as individual monuments—which in the late nineteenth century was particularly apposite given that so many of the objects existed in the public imagination within the gallery context—for the archaeologist the sculpture could only be an appropriate object of study when considered as a 'corpus' (Hawkes 2007, 150).

This perhaps identifies the fundamental tension between archaeologists and art historians concerning pre-Conquest sculpture. Archaeological methodology is usually reliant on large (and often diverse) datasets, while art historical approaches facilitate interrogation of individual objects. Thus, archaeological research is often criticized by art historians for its generalizing paradigms and art history is challenged by archaeologists for its inherent specificity. Nonetheless, influenced by Collingwood's methodology, many scholars have embraced style- and iconographic analysis, contributing to identification and interpretation of sculptural patronage, regional schools and the relationship(s) between visual and literary culture.

The Scottish, Welsh and Irish surveys of pre-Conquest sculpture (see above, pp. 4, 8) also interpret style as a temporal construct. As discussed above, late twentieth-century scholarship, informed by the methodologies explicit in such volumes, often refined dating chronologies through style-analysis, with resultant modifications sometimes eliciting new interpretations of stone sculptures. Lang's reassessment of the Jellinge-style zoomorph on "Middleton 2" (YN), for example (see above, p. 5), post-dated the monument to the tenth century; it also reaffirmed his contention that the cross's figural panel referenced secular lordship rather than pagan burial (Lang 1973, passim). Others, including Cramp, demonstrated that style can preserve evidence of culture-contact (Cramp 1977, passim; and Lang 1978, passim); whereas style's association with particular regions and schools has been explored by Bailey, Cramp, Sidebottom, Everson and Stocker, among others (Bailey 1980, 176-206, esp. 189-206; Cramp, "Anglian-Period Ornament", in Cramp and Bailey 1988, passim; Sidebottom 1999, 206-219, esp. 209 ff.; and Everson and Stocker 1999, 35-46).

Some of the most recent studies of Anglo-Saxon sculpture interpret the material iconologically, contextualizing typological data through extant cultural references. This approach is particularly useful for elucidating figural programmes and is advanced by Éamonn Ó Carragáin, Catherine Karkov, Jennifer O'Reilly and Jane Hawkes (Ó Carragáin 1978, passim; idem, 1986, passim; Karkov 2003, passim; O'Reilly 1993, passim; idem 1994, passim; Hawkes 1999, 403-421, esp. 405; and idem (2002, passim). However, in the context of Britain's and Ireland's early medieval stone sculpture, such researchers have apparently defined "cultural references" almost exclusively as literature, suggesting that other expressions of culture—including material and onomastic—are somehow less informative or reliable when employed as comparative and/or contextualizing evidence for carved stone. While the decoration of some sculptural groups (East Anglia's pre-Conquest funerary markers for example) can be interpreted thematically through contemporary literature, specific associations between text and motif are often not supported; thus, in the context of this prevailing, restrictive, definition of "iconology", some carvings, including the East Anglian examples, cannot be interrogated "iconologically" (Reed 2008, 181-182, 209-237).

The decoration of much pre-Conquest sculpture can, however, be interpreted "iconographically", informed by semiotic theory (Mynor 1994, 171-182; and Carter 1990, 66-94). However, as Sidebottom has suggested, stylistic (in)consistency (including the absence or presence of specific motifs, motif-combinations and spatial relationships), should not be universally interpreted as a fixed point on a typological continuum; it can also reflect regional distinctiveness, independent of presumed chronologies (Sidebottom 1999, 209).

Conclusion

It has been observed that England's pre-Conquest stone monuments are unique historical artifacts (Bailey 1980, 22; idem 1997, 12-13). Acknowledging their general immobility, such objects have rarely been disassociated from their original contexts; as such, they are important records of local and regional taste and of the social, religious and economic *milieux* informing their production and resultant styles (ibid., 22; 12). As public art, stone sculpture is also invaluable to elucidating identity and the apparent semiotic systems through which it is negotiated, expressed and understood.

Throughout its history, the study of pre-Conquest stone sculpture has been informed by both archaeological and art-historical methodologies. Despite the resultant tension arising from the disciplines' emphases on the general and the specific, respectively, archaeologists and art historians, together, have succeeded in elucidating many of the fundamental issues related to pre-Conquest stone monuments, including manufacture, patronage, decoration and function(s). This clearly demonstrates that interdisciplinary methodology is not only beneficial but *essential* to the study of England's early medieval sculpture.

Acknowledgements

I am grateful to Malcolm Thurlby for his comments on this paper.

Bibliography

Allen, J. and Anderson, J. [1903] 1993. *The Early Christian Monuments of Scotland*, 2 vols., Pinkfoot Press (Balgavies, Angus)

Almgren, B. 1955. *Bronsnycklar och djurornametik vid overgången från vendeltid till vikingatid*, Appelbergs boktr (Uppsala)

Arnold, T. (ed.) 1882-1885. *Symeonis Monachi Opera Omnia*, 2 vols., Rolls series 75 (London)

Bailey, R.N. 1978. "The Chronology of Viking-Age Sculpture in Northumbria", in J.T. Lang (ed.), *Anglo-Saxon and Viking Age Sculpture and its Context: papers from the Collingwood Symposium on insular sculpture from 800 to 1066*, B.A.R., British Series, 49 (Oxford): 173-203

Bailey, R.N. 1980. *Viking Age Sculpture in Northern England*, Collins (London)

Bailey, R.N. 1997. *England's Earliest Sculptors*, Publications of the Dictionary of Old English 5, Pontifical Institute of Mediaeval Studies (Toronto)

Bailey, R.N. and Cramp, R. 1988. *Corpus of Anglo-Saxon Stone Sculpture, vol. 2: Cumberland, Westmorland and Lancashire North-of-the-Sands*, Oxford University Press (Oxford)

Bakka, E. 1958. *On the beginning of Salin's Style I in England*. Universitetet i Bergen Årbok, Historiskantikvarisk Rekke III (Bergen)

Baldwin Brown, G. and Blyth Webster, A. 1921. *The Arts in Early England, vol. 5: The Ruthwell and Bewcastle Crosses the Gospels of Lindisfarne, and Other Christian Monuments of Northumbria*, John Murray (London)

Baldwin Brown, G. 1937. *The Arts in Early England, vol. 6, pt. ii: Anglo-Saxon Sculpture*, ed. E.H.L. Sexton, John Murray (London)

Bröndsted, J. 1924. *Early English Ornament: The Sources, Development and Relation to Foreign Styles of Pre-Norman Ornamental Art in England*, trans. A.F. Major, Hachette; Levin & Munksgaard (London; Copenhagen)

Camden, W. [1588] 1607. *Britannia* (London)

Carter, M. [1990] 1993. *Framing Art: Introducing Theory and the Visual Image*, Hale and Iremonger (Sydney)

Coatsworth, E. 2008. *Corpus of Anglo-Saxon Stone Sculpture, vol. 8: Western Yorkshire*, Oxford University Press (Oxford)

Collingwood, W.G. 1891. *The Art Teaching of John Ruskin*, Percival (London)

Collingwood, W.G. 1883. *The Philosophy of Ornament, eight lectures on the history of decorative Art, given at University college, Liverpool*, George Allen (Orpington)

Collingwood, W.G. 1907. "Anglian and Anglo-Danish sculpture in the North Riding of Yorkshire", *Yorkshire Archaeological Journal*, 19: 267-413

Collingwood, W.G. 1909. "Anglian and Anglo-Danish sculpture at York", *Yorkshire Archaeological Journal*, 20: 149-213

Collingwood, W.G. 1911. "Anglian and Anglo-Danish sculpture in the East Riding, with addenda relating to the North Riding", *Yorkshire Archaeological Journal*, 21: 254-302

Collingwood, W.G. 1916. "Anglian and Anglo-Danish sculpture in the West Riding, with addenda to the North and East Ridings and York, and a general review of the Early Christian monuments of Yorkshire", *Yorkshire Archaeological Journal*, 23: 129-299

Collingwood, W.G. [1927] 1989. *Northumbrian Crosses of the Pre-Norman Age*, Llanerch Enterprises (Felinfach, Powys)

Cramp, R. 1977. "Schools of Mercian Sculpture", in A. Dornier (ed.), *Mercian Studies*, Leicester University Press (Leicester): 191-233

Cramp, R. 1984. *Corpus of Anglo-Saxon Stone Sculpture, vol. 1: County Durham and Northumberland*, 2 pts., Oxford University Press (Oxford)

Cramp, R. [1984] 1991. *Grammar of Anglo-Saxon Ornament: A General Introduction to the Corpus of Anglo-Saxon Stone Sculpture*, Oxford University Press (Oxford)

Cramp, R. 1988. "Anglian Period Ornament", in R.N. Bailey and R. Cramp, *Corpus of Anglo-Saxon Stone Sculpture, vol. 2: Cumberland, Westmorland and Lancashire North-of-the-Sands*, Oxford University Press (Oxford): 15-18

Cramp, R. 2006. *Corpus of Anglo-Saxon Stone Sculpture, vol. 7: South-West England*, Oxford University Press (Oxford)

Evans, J. 1850. "On the date of British coins", *The Numismatic Chronicle and Journal of the Numismatic Society*, 12: 127-137

Everson, P. and Stocker, D. 1999. *Corpus of Anglo-Saxon Stone Sculpture, vol. 5: Lincolnshire*, Oxford University Press (Oxford)

Fernie, E. (ed.) 1995. *Art History and its Methods: a critical anthology*, Phaidon (London)

Geake, H. 1997. *The use of grave-goods in Conversion-period England, c. 600-c. 850*. B.A.R., British series, 261 (Oxford)

Hadley, D.M. and Richards, J.D. (eds.) 2000a. *Cultures in Contact: Scandinavian Settlement in England in the Ninth and Tenth Centuries*. Brepols (Turnhout, Belgium)

Hadley, D.M. and Richards, J.D. 2000b. "Introduction: interdisciplinary approaches to the Scandinavian settlement", in D.M. Hadley and J.D. Richards (eds.), *Cultures in Contact: Scandinavian Settlement in England in the Ninth and Tenth Centuries*, Brepols (Turnhout, Belgium): 3-15

Hawkes, J. 1999. "Statements in Stone: Anglo-Saxon Sculpture, Whitby and the Christianization of the North", in C. Karkov (ed.), *The Archaeology of Anglo-Saxon England: Basic Readings*, Garland (New York; London): 403-421

Hawkes, J. 2002. *The Sandbach Crosses: Sign and Significance in Anglo-Saxon Sculpture*, Four Courts Press (Dublin)

Hawkes, J. 2007. "Collingwood and Anglo-Saxon sculpture: art history or archaeology?", in R. Moss (ed.), *Making and Meaning in Insular Art: Proceedings of the fifth international conference on Insular art held at Trinity College Dublin, 25-28 August 2005*, Triarc Research Studies in Irish Art (Dublin): 142-152

Henry, F. [1940] 1965. *Irish Art in the Early Christian Period (to 800 A.D.)*, Methuen (London)

Henry, F. 1964. *Irish High Crosses*, Three Candles (Dublin)

Johnson, M. [1999] 2000. *Archaeological Theory: An Introduction*, Oxford University Press (Oxford)

Karkov, C. 2003. "Naming and Renaming: The Inscription of Gender in Anglo-Saxon Sculpture", in C. Karkov and F. Orton (eds.), *Theorizing Anglo-Saxon Stone Sculpture*, West Virginia University Press (Morgantown, West Virginia): 31-64

Lang, J.T. 1973. "Some late pre-Conquest crosses in Ryedale, Yorkshire: a re-appraisal", *Journal of the British Archaeological Association*, 36: 16-25

Lang, J.T. 1978. "Continuity and Innovation in Anglo-Scandinavian Sculpture: A Study of the Metropolitan School at York", in J.T. Lang (ed.), *Anglo-Saxon and Viking Age Sculpture and its Context: papers from the Collingwood Symposium on insular sculpture from 800 to 1066*, B.A.R., British Series, 49 (Oxford): 145-172

Lang, J.T. 2002. *Corpus of Anglo-Saxon Stone Sculpture, vol. 6: Northern Yorkshire*, Oxford University Press (Oxford)

Lang, J.T. et al. 1991. *Corpus of Anglo-Saxon Stone Sculpture, vol. 3: York and Eastern Yorkshire*, Oxford University Press (Oxford)

Lavell, C. and Wood, E. 1980. "Editors' Foreword", in R.N. Bailey, *Viking Age Sculpture*, Collins (London): v-vi

Lubbock, J. [1865] 1913. *Prehistoric times, as illustrated by ancient remains, and the manners and customs of modern savages*, Williams and Norgate (London)

Montelius, O. 1899. *Der Orient und Europa*, Selbstverlag des Verfassers (Stockholm)

Montelius, O. 1903. *Die typologische Methode: Die älteren Kulturperioden im Orient und in Europa*, Selbstverlag des Verfassers (Stockholm)

Morelli, G. 1892-1893. *Italian Painters: critical studies of their works*, 2 vols., trans. C. Ffoulkes, J. Murray (London)

Mynor, V. 1994. *Art History's History*, Prentice Hall (Englewood Cliffs, New Jersey)

Nash-Williams, V.E. 1950. *The Early Christian Monuments of Wales*, Wales University Press (Cardiff)

Ó Carragáin, É. 1978. "Liturgical Innovations Associated with Pope Sergius and the Iconography of the Ruthwell and Bewcastle Crosses", in R. Farrell (ed.), *Bede and Anglo-Saxon England*, B.A.R., British series, 46 (Oxford): 131-147

Ó Carragáin, É. 1986. "Christ over the Beasts and the Agnus Dei: Two Multivalent Panels on the Ruthwell and Bewcastle Crosses", in P. Szarmach and V. Oggins (eds.), *Sources of Anglo-Saxon Culture*, Studies in Medieval Culture 20, Medieval Institute Publications, Western Michigan University (Kalamazoo): 37-43

O'Reilly, J. 1993. "The Book of Kells, folio 114r: a Mystery Revealed yet Concealed", in R.M. Spearman and J. Higgitt (eds.), *The Age of Migrating Ideas: Early Medieval Art in Northern Britain and Ireland. Proceedings of the Second International Conference on Insular Art held in the National Museums of Scotland in Edinburgh, 3-6 January 1991*, National Museums of Scotland; Sutton (Edinburgh; Stroud): 106-114

O'Reilly, J. 1994. "Exegesis and the Book of Kells: the Lucan Genealogy", in F. O'Mahony (ed.), *The Book of Kells: Proceedings of a Conference at Trinity College Dublin, 6-9 September 1992*, Scholar Press (Aldershot): 344-397

Orton, F. 1999. "Northumbrian sculpture (the Ruthwell and Bewcastle monuments): questions of difference", in J. Hawkes and S. Mills (eds.), *Northumbria's Golden Age*, Sutton (Stroud, Gloucestershire): 216-226

Reed, M.F. 2008. *Sculpture and Identity in Late Saxon East Anglia*, 2 vols., unpublished Ph.D. dissertation, University of York, U.K.

Ruskin, J. 1905. "The two paths", §28-30, in E. Cook and A. Wedderburn (eds.), *Library Edition: the works of John Ruskin, vol. 16: 'A joy forever' and 'The two paths' with letters on the Oxford Museum and various addresses, 1856-60*, George Allen (London): 274-275

Ruskin, J. 1908. "The pleasures of England", lecture I: "The pleasures of learning", §28-29, in E. Cook and A. Wedderburn (eds.), *Library Edition: the works of John Ruskin, vol. 33: Bible of Amiens, Valle Crucis, Art of England, The Pleasures of England*, George Allen (London): 435-436

Salin, B. 1904. *Die altgermanische thierornamentik: typologische studie über germanische metallgegenstände aus dem IV. bis IX. jahrhundert, nebst einer studie über irische ornamentik*, K.L Beckmans büchdruckerei; A. Asher (Stockholm; Berlin)

Sidebottom, P. 1999. "Stone Crosses of the Peak and the 'Sons of Eadwulf'", *Derbyshire Archaeological Journal*, 119: 206-219

Stevens, W.O. 1904. *The Cross in the Life and Literature of the Anglo-Saxons*, Yale Studies in English 23, Henry Holt (New York)

Stocker, D. 2000. "Monuments and merchants: Irregularities in the distribution of stone sculpture in Lincolnshire and Yorkshire in the Tenth Century", in D.M Hadley and J.D. Richards (eds.), *Cultures in Contact: Scandinavian Settlement in England in the Ninth and Tenth Centuries*, Brepols (Turnhout, Belgium): 179-212

Stubbs, W. (ed.) 1887. *Willelmi Malmesbiriensis Monachi de Gestis Regum Anglorum*, 2 vols., Rolls series 90 (London)

Thomsen, C. 1836. *Ledetraad til Nordisk Oldkyndighed*, Kjøb (Copenhagen)

Toulmin-Smith, T. (ed.) 1906-1910. *The Itinerary of John Leland in England and Wales*, 5 vols., (London)

Trigger, B. [1989] 2006. *A History of Archaeological Thought*, Cambridge University Press (Cambridge)
Tweddle, D. *et al.* 1995. *Corpus of Anglo-Saxon Stone Sculpture, vol. 4: South-East England*, Oxford University Press (Oxford)

Wicker, N. 1999. "Archaeology and Art History: Common ground for the New Millennium", *Medieval Archaeology*, 43: 161-171

Wilson, D.M. 1959. "Almgren and Chronology: A Summary and some Comments", *Medieval Archaeology*, 3: 112-119

Worsaae, J. 1849. *The primeval antiquities of Denmark*, trans. W. Thoms, J.H. Parker (London)

Another Perspective on the Origins and Symbolic Interpretations of Animals in Early Medieval Sculpture in Northern England and French Burgundy

Nicole M. Kleinsmith, Ph.D.
Independent Scholar, Santa Barbara, California

Introduction

To date, the symbolic significance of animals in early medieval western European sculpture has been generally understudied. The analysis of carvings of pre-Norman origin focuses primarily on their dating, style and possible connection to particular schools of sculpture. Additionally, the iconographic exemplars of these carved images are usually identified as portable objects, including metal artifacts, illuminated manuscripts and cloths and tapestries of various origins, including Greco-Roman, Sassanian, Celtic, Norse and Anglo-Saxon.[1] Although these assessments are invaluable as departure points for any research into the possible symbolism of artifacts, they have resulted, too frequently, in the labelling of sculptures as "decorative", the dismissal of their iconography as incomprehensible and/or the declaration by researchers that the imagery is beyond their area of interest.[2] As a result, scholars have been reluctant to admit the possibility that pre-Christian themes related to the survival or revival of pagan worship may be depicted on sculpture due, primarily, to the objects' placement in, or association with, Christian buildings. While difficult to investigate, the symbolic significance of these images deserves inquiry beyond the established frames of reference.[3] Accordingly, it is relevant to explore the commonality between some representations on sculptural elements found in, and/or near, early medieval Insular and Continental churches, and the art forms and artifacts associated with the latent belief in, and the ritualistic worship of, ancient Celtic, Germanic, Gallic and Norse deities. Despite difficulties extricating these ancestral beliefs, there is little doubt that they lingered in the collective memory of the medieval public.[4] Indeed, medieval texts contain references to the Christian Church's preoccupation with alternative religious practices, acknowledged under the blanket term of *superstitiones*.[5] Yet, contemporary writings directly related to these sculptures and their meanings are not extant. Nevertheless, medieval texts address existing preoccupation with the open display of alternative religious beliefs and rituals. In the British Isles, the ecclesiastical canons of King Edgar (AD 959) exhort Christian priests to "zealously promote Christianity" and enjoin the people to renounce "vain practices". On the continent, Hincmar, the ninth-century Bishop of Reims was more specific when he enjoined his flock against what he termed "*turpia ioca cum urso*" (Migne 1879, *P.L.*, CXXV, 776). In his repetition of Hincmar's admonitions a century later, Regino de Prüm demonstrated the clergy's continuing concern.[6] In many cases, what is known today about pre-Christian rites and practices has been subsumed and transformed, reaching us through the filters of mythological tales and folkloric performances. Yet, as J.C. Schmitt states, in the Early Middle Ages, these ancestral beliefs were part of "… the network of symbols woven by liturgy in sacred space and in calendar time" (Schmitt 1998, 383).

This article is intended only as an introduction to a rich area of research. It focuses primarily on the possible symbolic meanings of some animals, such as the boar, the swan/goose, and the bear with his "human" avatars the wild man/green man. These figural representations are depicted in the decoration of Insular stone funerary monuments, known as hogbacks, in Nottinghamshire and North Yorkshire (*ca* 950-1050), on a plaque from Cumbria (early tenth-century), and on several Continental (Burgundian) capitals (*ca* 1000-1130). An examination of these carved images found in different geographic areas reveals a common background for the themes, despite variations in their representations. What is depicted suggests the continued existence of a pre-Christian schema in a Christian environment slowly evolving towards intolerance (Soufflet 1981, passim). It is interesting to note that despite cultural and religious exchanges between the British Isles and the Continent, variations may be noted between the rituals represented and the manner in which pre-Christian *superstitiones* were introduced into the sculptural designs. The fact that these two geographic areas had firmly entrenched pre-Christian roots was also considered, since remnants of

---

[1] Much has been written on the sources of decoration for carved stone. See Adhémar (1996, passim, esp. 156-57); Basford (1978, 9); Deschamps (1925, 5-28); Evans, (1950, 46-121); Grodecki (1986, 85-86); Petzold (1995, 12-14, 50); Zarnecki (1979, 168-189).
[2] For possible origins of early medieval sculptures, see Bailey (1986, 14); Camus, M.T. (1992, 104-105); Evans (1950, 46-121); Hearn (1981, 42, 125); Grodecki. (1986, 88); Zarnecki (1979, 168).
[3] For the symbolic significance of images, especially animal representations in the art of the Early Middle Ages, see Voisenet (1994, 136-200).
[4] For enduring pre-Christian practices and rituals in medieval society, see Boglioni, (1983, 349-52); Laliberté (2000, 19-36).
[5] For pre-Christian religion and its survival and revival, see Schmitt (1988, 1, 425, 429, 441-42, 499-504); Laliberté (2000, 220).
[6] For a discussion of these concerns, which continued well into the Middle Ages, see Bernhiemer (1952, 54-55).

pagan rituals and the worship of pre-Christian deities survived well into the Middle Ages, albeit in a Christianized form, later demonized, ostracized, and transformed into myths, devolving into folklore. But why choose two such apparently disparate geographic areas?

The choice of Insular and Continental locales was the result of a study of the confluence of political, economic, cultural and religious interests that may have made it permissible, and perhaps even necessary, to accommodate pre-Christian images in Christian settings, such as churches and their associated burial grounds. This choice was also the result of an evaluation of the themes represented in extant early medieval sculptures that may be linked to pre-Christian beliefs.

Background

At the dawn of the second millennium, the numerous victories realised by pagan invaders, over an often minimally Christianized local populace, were instrumental in rekindling an interest in pre-Christian ritual practices, which had never completely disappeared.[7] The destruction and pillaging of Christian centers by pagan invaders had interrupted production of architectural and sculptural works in stone (Cook and Herzman 1983, 225-26). Yet, by the mid-tenth century, the invaders had begun to settle in their new environments.[8] The establishment of political stability in Europe favoured economic growth, facilitating the rebuilding of ecclesiastical centers in more durable materials. Commenting on Anglo-Scandinavian sculpture in Yorkshire, James Lang notes that "the reason for the *floruit* was undoubtedly the growing prosperity of York as a commercial center" (Lang 1978, 20). The architectural and sculptural works remaining from the tenth and eleventh centuries were often incorporated into later constructions in successive building campaigns.

Religion and Figural Representations: Inclusion or Exclusion?

Compounding the problems at the local level, the Christian Church had fallen into a state of disarray. Starting with the reign of Pope Nicholas I (867), and lasting until the election of Pope Leo VIII (963), a dissolute clergy, rife with corruption, gave rise to wandering monks and false prophets who added their heretical teachings to the plethora of beliefs and *superstitiones*.[9] In the British Isles, however, saintly men who followed the Benedictine Rule, adopted by Cluny, such as Wilfrid, Bishop of York (late seventh/early eighth centuries) and Dunstan, Archbishop of Canterbury (*ca* 960-988) endeavoured to maintain, and then to reform, the Church. A sense of collective helplessness is reflected in the words of the famous cleric Alcuin after the attack on Lindisfarne in 793: "... What assurance is there for the churches of Britain, if St. Cuthbert with so great a number of saints, defends not his own?" (Whitelock 1955, 776). Alcuin's statement reflects the perceived power that the early medieval public placed in saints' relics. Indeed, it was believed that during troubled periods, relics could strengthen public authority, protecting and securing communities, and providing economic prosperity. Because they were considered an extension of a saint's person, relics were honoured as a continuing presence and a manifestation of the person as "alive" and "active".[10] It was believed that through the intrinsic power of his/her relic, a saint was able to participate in the life of a city.[11] However, in order to be accepted as a truly worthy remnant of a saint, a relic had to prove itself by performing miracles. For such miracles to continue, veneration of the relic was required.[12] With the destruction of Lindisfarne, Alcuin voiced his doubt in the efficacy of St Cuthbert's relics. If the faith of such a man as Alcuin was shaken, what can be said of the faith of the *rustici*?

On the Continent, the situation was similar. In addition to feelings of betrayal by the Church, its bishops and its priests, the *rustici*, who represented the majority of the early medieval population, felt abandoned by the saints and their relics. As a result, they were amenable to revisit forms of pagan practice and/or were receptive to the beliefs of pagan raiders. Their religious faith and associated methods of worship were often eclectic, intermixing Christian, heretical Christian (remnants of Pelagianism in the British Isles) and/or pre-Christian polytheism. The clergy was forced to compromise if the Church was to survive. Indeed, it became a matter of necessity for the Church to alter and/or appropriate whatever seemed useful in its fight for the continued salvation of human souls. But, how were the clerics to proceed? Is it possible that in their yearning to convey Christian ideas, clerics permitted the inter-mixing of pre-Christian and Christian iconography?

---

[7] For the political and cultural developments and their influences on Insular society, see Cahill (1995, 158); Johnson (1985, 13-67, 107-108). See also Schmitt, (1988, 429), especially for Continental society.

[8] For Insular history, see Johnson (1985, 13-67); McLynn (1999, xiii); Sawyer (1978, passim); Smyth (1978, passim). For the history of Continental Europe from 480-1180, see Le Jan (1996, passim, esp. 137). For the interactions of Vikings and Celts, see Renaud (1992, passim).

[9] For heretical teachings and false prophets, see Chélini (1997, 106-108); Le Jan (1996, 161-62); Schnürer (1935, 94-98). For the rule of St Benedict, which mentions "gyratory" monks and their false teachings, see Henderson (1965, 275).

[10] According to Geary (1986, 174), "relics were the saints continuing to live among men"; ibid (176), "In the West ... their corpses [the saints'] were seen as the *pignora*, literally, the security deposits left by the saints upon their deaths as guarantees of their continuing interest in the earthly community".

[11] According to Sumpton (1975, 4), "Contempt for the relics of the saints were regularly visited with dumbness, bodily distortion, disease, madness, and death". Geary (1986, 171) also mentions that "they [relics] were immediate sources of supernatural power for good and for ill, and close contact with them or possession of them was a means of participating in that power".

[12] Quoting St Bernard of Clairvaux, Sumpton (1975, 53) mentions Bernard's complaint that the relics were worshipped as "Jupiter or Mars might well have been venerated ...".

In that regard, it is interesting to note the influence demonstrated by Christian reformers (mid-tenth to late twelfth centuries), especially by the Cluny-trained Benedictine clerics, who traveled far and wide in their effort to breathe new life into the Church. As noted below, changes incorporated into the Christian liturgy, as well as in the architectural and sculptural programs that these clerics sought to implement, evidenced their desire for reform. From the early years of the Christian era, clerics had struggled with a state of ambivalence *vis à vis* the use of images in religious contexts. Images exert a powerful attraction, especially on the illiterate. Because the early Church Fathers feared that images would rekindle the newly Christianized people's attachment to their past superstitions and would foster strong connections to pre-Christian forms of worship, they forbade figural representations within Christian spaces and regarded the destruction of pagan images as a Christian duty (Adhémar 1996, 82 and n. 2; Miquel and Picard 1997, 399; Voisenet 1994, 259-61; Thornton 1986, passim). Yet, concessions were made. Christian clerics acknowledged that pagan buildings and *spolia* could be rendered safe if crosses were inscribed on them and if *spolia* were installed in courses along walls as apotropaic defences. A similar state of ambivalence continued to reign in the Church. Pope Gregory the Great (590-604) strongly supported the use of images to educate the illiterate, while missionaries were still admonishing the *rustici* to distance themselves from idol worship.[13] In 1025, during a synod convened at Arras, a group of bishops and abbots reiterated Gregory's mandate, which points to the continued struggle between those who supported the use of images and the iconoclasts (Davy 1977, 113). However, the proliferation of sculpted elements in Christian settings, dating from the mid-tenth to the twelfth century and beyond, points to an enthusiastic response to Gregory's mandate. Yet, uncertainty as to which approach to follow continued.

Decisions regarding the inclusion or exclusion of figural representations remained a persistent problem for medieval clerics.[14] Feeling that the time was past for forced conversion en masse "à la Charlemagne", these clerics could no longer ignore their role as educators of the masses; nor could they fail to address and attempt to redress the contentious beliefs, the *superstitiones*, of the *pagani* and *rustici* (Schmitt 1988, 502). In the twelfth century, although Bernard of Clairvaux vituperated against the inclusion of "ridiculous monstrosities" in his monasteries, he seems to have appreciated the dilemma facing the Church. Indeed, Bernard wrote that "... bishops have one kind of business and monks another ...

Since they [the bishops] are responsible for both the wise and the foolish, they [the bishops] stimulate the devotion of a carnal people with material ornaments because they cannot do so with spiritual ones".[15] Such statements demonstrate a continued underlying need to steer the public towards more orthodox Christian beliefs, probably in part because of the survival and/or revival of pre-Christian popular beliefs in contemporary culture.[16] They also point to the desire of the early medieval Church to fulfill a missionary role, which is to educate. Repression, oppression and license for official violence were legitimized beginning in the late twelfth century.[17]

Survival/Revival: Pre-Christian Beliefs and Rituals and the Early Medieval Public

While investigating the symbolism of early medieval sculptural themes, it is necessary to acknowledge that images both affect and reflect trends, mores and customs and attempt to understand what cultural and religious influences were brought to bear on the early medieval sculptors. The early medieval *rustici*, like the agrarian societies of the ancient world, believed in the supernatural powers of images.[18] Gaignebet and Florentin noted the intentional preservation, conversion and internalization of pre-Christian rituals, symbology and practices when they stated that "it is evident that Christian liturgy preserved and appropriated a whole series of pre-Christian elements" (Gaignebet and Florentin 1979, 55).

One of these was the perception of time which differed markedly from our own. For the pagan Celts, Germans (Anglo-Saxon and Franks) and Scandinavians, time was not linear but cyclical, each cycle evolving in pendular fashion from one extreme to the other (shortest day to longest and back again). Any change from one season to another was considered dangerous, since the barrier between the human world and the *Sid* (the world inhabited by the gods) became fluid. This permeability could involve passing from one season to another or from human time into the timelessness of the Gods. It also meant passing from one state to another (life to death in the fall, death to life in the spring) and from one species to another, since medieval people, even the erudite, believed in fertilization across species (from animal to human and vice versa).[19] Each passage was marked by a feast day accompanied by ritualistic ceremonies. There is

---

[13] In a *Vita* of St Amand (7th c.), the saint demands that a blind woman cut down a tree inhabited by spirits in order to recover her sight. A very rare representation of this event is portrayed in the twelfth-century *Vie et Miracle de Saint Amand* (F. 119, MS 501, Valenciennes, Bibliothèque municipale), illustrated in Gaignebet and Lajoux (1985, 76). For Gregory the Great's recommendations, see Davy (1977, 112) and Grabar ([1979] 1994, 32).
[14] According to Voisenet (1994, 171), "les clercs procèdent à un savant dosage entre une oblitération et une récupération partielle de la figure animale".

[15] See Rudolph's (1990, 10-12) translation of Bernard of Clairvaux's (1095-1153) *Apologia ad Gillelmum*, pt. 28-29.
[16] For popular religion, see Gaignebet and Lajoux. (1985, passim); Plongeron (1976, passim); Duboscq, et al. (1979, passim); Bolgiani (1981, passim); Lauwers (1990, passim). This list is not exhaustive.
[17] For sanctioning violence as a means of eradicating pre-Christian beliefs, see Little and Rosenwein (1998, "Introduction to Part IV", 307); Moore (1977, passim); and Moore (1987, passim).
[18] For the re-use of pagan images, see James (1996, 16); and Mango (1984, 59-61).
[19] For the concept of time in early medieval society, see Gaignebet and Lajoux. (1985, 83). For the beliefs in fertilization across species, which accounted for monstrous birth, see Dontenville (1966, 65-85).

little doubt that these beliefs persisted either as survivals or as revivals.

Why, then, focus on representations of animals, especially the bear and his avatars, the wild man/green man? According to ancient mythology, the bear was significant in early societies (Brunner 2007, 10; Lajoux 1996, passim; Pastoureau 2002, 150-54; Praneuf 1989, passim).[20] For the pre-Christian Celtic, Germanic (Anglo-Saxon and Franks), and Scandinavian peoples, the bear functioned as an intermediary between the material world, subjected to human time, and the world of the gods, independent of human time (Becker (1994, 37). Like other animals, such as the goose, often conflated with the swan, bears functioned as messengers to the gods and as psychopomps, that is, keepers and carriers of souls (Chevalier and Gheerbrant 2000, 694, 716-18). Since the Celts considered the white swan/goose a symbol of purity and light, Christian clerics could assimilate Celtic symbolism with their own when attempting to explain the Holy Spirit to the *rustici* (Thibaud 1995, 111). Additionally, as king of animals, the bear was the emblem of the ruler and of the warrior class, unlike the boar that symbolized the priestly class.[21] In fact, the belief in the bear, as king of the animals, survived well into the Middle Ages, before the lion dethroned him (Pastoureau 2007, passim; idem 2002, 153).

The bear was also the companion of *Artio* (from the Celtic root "art" meaning "bear"), the divinity of the hunt and death in the Gallo-Celtic pantheon (Chevalier and Gheerbrant 2000, 716-17 ; MacKillop 2004, 25, 36; Thibaud 1995, 33, 302-03). A Gallo-Celtic bronze statue, dating from the first century BC, represents a large bear holding at bay the goddess Artio (life holding death at bay). Artio sits impassively, slightly recoiled. This recoiling from the advancing bear may intimate that even death feared the bear, since he functions as the guardian of life, symbolized by the bear touching the trunk of a tree from which several leaves sprout.[22] It was believed that, as keeper of the souls of the dead of all species (vegetal, animal and human), the bear carried these essences within him when he "died", entering his den in the fall (Celtic feast of *Samane*, Nov. 1st and 2nd).

The clergy, especially the monks and their abbots, who lived in large abbeys in rural settings surrounded by the natural world, were not immune to these influences. Indeed, the Christian calendar reflects an adoption and adaptation of pre-Christian feast days. While the feast of All Saints had a long history dating back to the first century of Christian worship, it was celebrated at different dates in various places (Foy 1981, 278; Walsh 1998, 359-60). In 835, under Germano-Gallic influence, Pope Gregory IV (827-844) fixed the feast of All Saints on November 1st (Pietri 1988, 25-26, 57-61; Walsh 1998, 88-89). Subsequently, in 998, St Odilo, the third abbot of Cluny, appropriated the remaining part of the pre-Christian feast of *Samane*, transforming it into All Souls' Day, the feast of the dead. Henceforth, in the Western Church, the dead were remembered solemnly on Nov. 2nd.[23] In addition, the Benedictine Order of Cluny seems to have engaged in a deliberate attempt to strengthen the connection between the Church and pre-Christian beliefs and rituals, especially those associated with the bear/wild man, which was even reflected in their attire.[24] As described by Adalbéron, Bishop of Laon (died *ca* 1030), the monks covered their heads with "un grand bonnet fait de la peau d'une ourse de Lybie", as part of their ceremonial winter attire (Hückel 1901, passim).

When the bear awakened from hibernation and was "reborn" at the beginning of the Celtic Spring (feast of *Imbolc*, Feb. 2nd),[25] he released the souls that had been in his care during hibernation, thus enabling the greenery to re-emerge from the earth.[26] In the pre-Christian calendar, May 1st was the beginning of summer. *Beltane* was celebrated on this day, the feast of the god who brought the earth back to life with his benevolent light and warm breath.[27] How can one explain the transformation of the bear (awakened at *Imbolc*) into the wild man/green man most often found in the celebration of the feast of *Beltane*?

It is interesting to note that the wild man emerges for the first time as a distinct character from the pages of the *History of the East*, written by Herodotus (fifth century B.C). In this treatise, the wild man is mentioned as belonging to the monstrous races that dwelled in Libya, a country believed then to be on the edge of the world.[28] Is it a coincidence that Adalbéron assigns Libya as the origin for the large bear skin hoods worn by the Cluniacs? Did the medieval public, erudite and *rustici* alike, consider the bear and wild man/green man interchangeable?

---

[20] Remains of ritualistically arranged bear bones and skulls have been found in many European caves, see Gaignebet and Lajoux (1985, 80, 238-58).

[21] Thibaud (1995, 303) explains that "dans les mythes celtes, l'Ours est toujours opposé au Sanglier qui représente la function sacerdotale, le pouvoir spirituel des druides et des pretres". See also Cazenave (1996, 490).

[22] A photograph of this small statue (25 cm high), with the inscription "*DEAE ARTIONI /LICINIA SABINILLA*" on its base, is reproduced in Guyonvarc'h and Le Roux (1990, fig. 9). A drawing of this statue is reproduced in Green (1989, 28).

[23] Gaignebet and Lajoux (1985, 255); Iogna-Prat (1998, 221), quotes the *Liber tramitis aevi Odilonis*, in Dinter (ed.). *Corpus consuetudinum monasticarum* (1980, 10/126:186-87, and 10/138: 199); idem (1998, 341); Jones (1995, 194).

[24] Schmitt (1988, 502) notes that "il fallut adapter le langage de l'Eglise à chaque groupe particulier ...".

[25] Le Roux and Guyonvarc'h (1995, 83) define *Imbolc* as "une lustration ou une purification au sortir des rigueurs de l'hiver". It is interesting to note that in the Christian calendar, Feb. 2nd is the feast of the Purification of the Virgin.

[26] For the Celtic feasts of *Samane, Imbolc*, and *Beltane* see Guyonvarc'h and Le Roux (1986, 258-59); Guyonvarc'h and Le Roux (1990, 162-63); Le Roux and Guyonvarc'h (1995, 83-86); Thibaud (1995, 209, 340). For the role of the bear at *Imbolc*, see Gaignebet and Lajoux (1985, 261); Thibaud (1995, 313-14).

[27] *Beltane* is derived from the Irish Gaelic *Bealtaine* or the Scottish Gaelic *Bealtuinn*. *Beltane* is named after *Belenos*, the Celtic god of light (also Bel, Beli or Belinus), who brings life and the greening of the world.

[28] For a reference to the origins of the wild man in Herodotus' *The Marvels of the East*, see Bernheimer (1952, 86); Husband (1980, 5-6).

When bears were no longer found readily, a man would be dressed in a furry costume to play the role of the bear and to reenact ritually the bear's "death", a practice that survives in European folklore (Gaignebet and Lajoux 1985, 154-57; Van Gennep 1947, passim; idem 1960, 910). In the distant past, the feast of *Beltane* may have included human sacrifice. However, this simple explanation may only be the outward, practical solution to a complex interchange because, firmly believing in "*le merveilleux*" (Chélini 1997, 357; *Meslin* 1984, *passim*), medieval people were convinced that fertilization across species was possible (Dontenville 1966, 65-85; Gaignebet and Lajoux 1985, 83). This concept helped explain occurrences of abnormal births, deformities in both animals and humans and justified mental illness. Educated and literate people acknowledged the existence of monsters, fantastic beings, and monstrous races and discussed their nature and the place that they held in the Christian order of the universe.[29] Also, Bernheimer notes that "the wild man's closest associates were bears" (Bernheimer 1952, 59). He elaborates that "bears and men were interchangeable, because the bear – the 'man of the woods' – may stand upright in its tracks like a man, while the wild man resembles it in his close-fitting fur", adding that "in rituals ... the distinction between man and beast is not always rigorously maintained" (Bernheimer 1952, 53-54).[30] Gaignebet and Lajoux concur with Bernheimer when they note that, "pour l'imaginaire médiéval l'homme et l'ours sont confondus" (Gaignebet and Lajoux 1985, 83).

From the evolution of pre-Christian beliefs into myths, later transformed into popular tales, another persona of the bear/wild man emerges. Some secular medieval writings recount the tales of a man who, raised and nursed by a she-bear, behaves like a wild man.[31] Brought back to civilization, and once shaved or liberated from his bear skin, this wild man emerges as a man, sometimes with a green skin, the color of new growth (Gaignebet and Lajoux 1985, 114-119). Conversely, men would dress in bear skins in the fall and in layers of leaves in the spring in order to emulate the bear and his avatars and to re-enact pre-Christian rituals celebrating the change of seasons. The ceremonies surrounding the death of winter and the birth of spring were deemed necessary to secure the release and prevent the wasting of souls that could deplete both human and animal species. It was an important ritual to ensure fertility and growth, a common concern of agrarian societies (Guyonvarc'h and Le Roux 1990, 160-63; Gaignebet and Lajoux 1985, 90, 255, 283-288; Le Roux and Guyonvarc'h 1995, 76-84, 165-176). The continued relevance of these rituals in the Middle Ages may be explained by the survival of pagan worship amongst "the profoundly pagan masses" (Muchembled 1985, 33).

The enduring nature of pre-Christian rituals can also be traced to the "basically animist view of the world" that permeated the primarily agrarian medieval culture (ibid., 29). In this respect, the inhabitants of the Danelaw in the British Isles or the Burgundians in France may have sought refuge in this profound, atavistic schema when exposed to violent changes in their lives. Extant mythological tales recounting the lives and exploits of heroic figures are mere reflections derived from ancient beliefs and the corruption of those beliefs. These factors should be acknowledged when considering the possible symbolic meanings of early medieval sculptures, whether Insular or Continental.

Early Medieval Insular Sculpture and its Symbolism

When examining early medieval Insular sculpture, one is immediately drawn to pre-Norman stone crosses. Indeed, the sculptural programs on tenth to twelfth century crosses in North Yorkshire impelled J.T. Lang to comment on how changes in the political, cultural and religious environments affected sculptural themes. Lang proposes that "in a sense this is art as propaganda, or it may simply be a need to establish continuity as a concept of the organization of the church at that time and in that place through the medium of monumental art" (Lang 1997, 69-71). In other words, the images on early medieval stone crosses might reflect the Church's need to assimilate competing beliefs at a particular time and that this integration was reflected in monumental sculpture. As mentioned above, the Church has generally been ambivalent about sculptural decoration in Christian settings. Yet, while "survival" and "revival" of styles and ateliers are discussed at length, and while their intricate carvings have been the focus of attention, many unresolved questions remain concerning the content and symbolism of such sculpture. Similar problems are encountered when studying sculptural forms other than stone crosses (Lang 2002, 20-27). Thus, this article focuses on one sculptural form, the hogback tomb/grave-marker and its decoration. Lang describes the hogback as follows:

> [It is] a housed-shaped recumbent monument of the Viking Age with a definitive curve to the roof ridge. The roof is usually tegulated and the gables are sometimes embraced by three-dimensional animals ... an innovation of tenth-century Norse-Irish settlers in Northern England ... The type originated in North Yorkshire about the second quarter of the tenth century and appears to have remained popular in the North Riding and Cumbria for only a short period (Lang 1972-4, 206-35).

Lang categorizes them by type and notes that "they often have three-dimensional end-beasts of bear-like appearance", and that "the form was short-lived, probably only a matter of some thirty years between the Hiberno-

---

[29] For a thorough discussion of monstrous, fantastic and exotic beings, see Lecouteux (1993, *passim*); Wittkower (1942, passim).
[30] For the interchangeability of man and bear, see Brunner (2007, 20).
[31] For references to Bear and Wild Man tales such as 'Valentin et Ourson', 'L'Homme à la peau d'ours', 'Jean de l'Ours', 'Jean de Fer', see Gaignebet and Lajoux (1985, 90).

Norse incursion of c. 920 and the English takeover in 954 ... ".[32] Lang concludes that the more naturalistic carvings are probably the earliest. He posits that the stylized versions of the end-beasts were produced later, before completely disappearing (Lang 1984, 97). Richard Bailey adopts the opposite chronology, contending that the stylized beast is the earliest (Bailey 1980, 97-98). In addition to his discussions of style and chronology, Lang acknowledges the "uncompromisingly secular or even pagan" appearance of these tenth-century funerary monuments (Lang 1978, 11). Klayman, who notes that the bears "convey a recollection of Scandinavia", assimilates "the muzzle feature" which relates "a passive complacency suitable to the English notion of civilization" to "a clear symbol of the taming and domestication of the wild warrior" (Klayman [1997] 2002, 4-5).

While possible, it is difficult to assign such meaning to the decoration of stone monuments used as grave-lids or -markers. It is also difficult to assert that the purpose for such sculptures, which Klayma states, "remains a great mystery to scholars, as does its short span of existence" (ibid., 1).[33] Considering the possible influence of Scandinavian myth on Viking-period stone sculpture in England, Bailey states that, "apart from a major find at York Minster ..., no new pieces which might be interpreted as depicting mythology have emerged" (Bailey 2000, 15). Yet, discussing the carvings on hogbacks, Lang is of the opinion that there is evidence of interaction between the pre-Christian Scandinavian and Christian Anglo-Saxon traditions (Lang 1978, 11). How can we reconcile these disparate opinions? Indeed, it should be noted that both in the British Isles and on the Continent, as late as the eleventh century, members of some noble families, including Earl Siward of Northumberland (d. 1055), the Danish King Svend Estridsen (1047-1074) and the Counts of Toulouse, believed they were descended from bears.[34]

Despite the scholarly disagreement mentioned above, the belief that some early medieval elites possessed ursine ancestry demonstrates the enduring nature of pre-Christian beliefs in their societies. There is little doubt that such beliefs influenced the decoration of sculpted artifacts.

The *Nwyvre* and the Bear from Hickling

Examination of select funerary monuments will demonstrate the significance of ursine associations in early medieval Insular culture. In the chancel of the Church of St Luke at Hickling near the Nottingham-Leicestershire border, two hogbacks are laid perpendicularly on supporting blocks along the chancel walls. One of the Hickling hogbacks is adorned with flat serpentine creatures of the *Jellinge* type, which are separated into square compartments by cross designs (fig. 1).[35] In the various compartments, beasts are caught within the swirling, sometimes knotted embrace of serpentine figures (fig. 2).

Fig. 1. Hickling. hogback with serpentine creatures and muzzled bear, ca mid-tenth century (© Rev. Chris Tolley).

Fig. 2. Hickling. Beast caught in the wyverns' embrace, ca mid-tenth century (© Rev. Chris Tolley).

The head, torso and upper limbs of a muzzled bear are also carved at each end of the monument (fig. 3). The bears' heads rest on the ridge of the hogback, while their front paws seem to be pushing down as though to keep it tightly shut (fig. 3). In view of the discussion above, what symbolism might be attributed to these carvings? In northwestern European mythology, especially in the Celtic belief system, the cosmos was formed of five elements: the four known elements of air, water, fire and earth, and a fifth known as the *Nwyvre* or wyvern, also known as the World-Serpent (Bailey 1996, 90-91). In Norse and Celtic mythology, this writhing element,

---

[32] See Lang (2002, 20); see also Lang (1991, 29). For the dating, see Bailey (2000, 19).
[33] Elaborating on the same subject, Stone ([1955]1972, 66-69) declared that the naturalistic end-beasts at Brompton should "... be treated as a more or less freak adventure in art, out of the main line of sculptural development and hopeless of posterity".
[34] Belief in animal ancestry, especially powerful animals, was widespread in the Middle Ages. For the British Isles, see Brunner (2007, 26); for the Continent, see Gaignebet and Lajoux (1985, 79).

[35] "*Jellinge*" refers to Jellinge in Jutland where this style of decoration was first discovered. Collingwood (1908, passim); Collingwood (1909a, passim). See also Fisher (1959, 76-80).

Fig. 3. Hickling. Enhanced photograph of muzzled bear (end of hogback), ca mid-tenth century (© Rev. Chris Tolley).

encompassing the universe, symbolized the creative force, a type of cosmic fluid or ether, as well as a creative and divine life force, which held the universe together.[36] It is embodied by a writhing serpent or a two-legged dragon known as the wyvern, which Marcel Moreau describes as "le fil reliant mystérieusement le monde humain au monde divin" (Moreau 1995, 59-60).[37] As discussed above, in the European pre-Christian belief system, the bear functioned as a psychopomp and as a liaison between the material world and the *Sid*. On the Hickling hogback, crosses proclaim the Christian Faith. Thus, a mixture of pre-Christian and Christian elements is united on the Hickling sculpture. Perhaps in his/her eagerness to ensure safe passage for the soul of the deceased, Hickling's tenth-century patron(s) incorporated both Christian and pagan references in the memorial's decorative program. The sculptor included serpentine creatures or the "fifth element" (*Nwyvre*), which binds life (symbolized by the various animals) together. He also depicted muzzled bears, perhaps ensuring that these dutiful guardians of souls would protect the deceased from harmful or even destructive influences. Crosses were also included in the stone's decoration, representing, in this newly-acquired belief system, the prelude to Christ's resurrection and the promised salvation of the Faithful. As mentioned above, while Christian clerics sought to disengage the *rustici* from their pagan beliefs, they were pragmatic in their approach. In his research on superstitious beliefs, J. C. Schmitt noted:

En matière de superstitions, les clercs firent ainsi des découvertes insoupçonnées. Dans les filets de leurs visites pastorales, de leurs tournées de prédication ou de leurs inquisitions, ils ramenèrent une masse d'informations d'une richesse sans précédent sur des légendes, des croyances, des rituels (Schmitt 1998, 502).

Sinnington

Additional examples of this adapting of religious traditions are extant in North Yorkshire. At All Saints' Church, Sinnington, many fragments of pre-Norman crosses and hogbacks were incorporated into the church fabric, rebuilt in the twelfth century.[38] These fragments are carved with intricate intertwined figures of serpents and wyverns, again symbolizing the *Nwyvre*, the life-giving and sustaining element (figs. 4a, 4b).

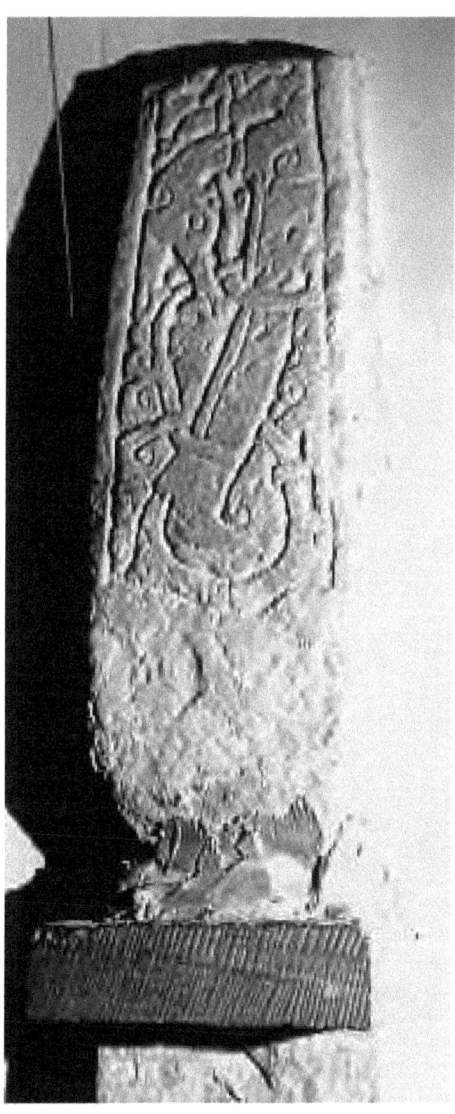

Fig. 4a. Sinnington. Nwyvre or wyvern (sculptural fragment installed on a wall of All Saints' Church), ca mid-tenth century (© Rev. Christ Tolley).

---

[36] It is interesting to note that twenty-first century scientists are actively involved in finding such cosmic "glue" which they have termed "dark matter", an elusive, yet according to recent findings, indispensable element in the structure of the Universe.

[37] In alchemy, the serpent is the *materia prima*; it is also equated with cosmogonic powers and the generative forces of chaos. See Cazenave (1996, 623, 629); Chevalier and Gheerbrant (2000, 869).

[38] Twenty one fragments of Anglo-Saxon sculptures were discovered during an early-twentieth-century restoration. See Bailey (1996, 11).

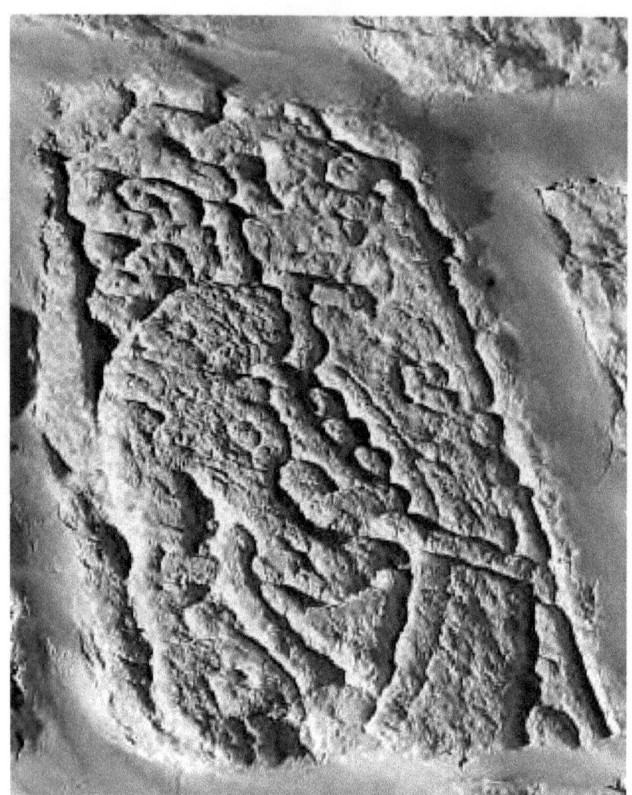

Fig. 4b. Sinnington. Nwyvre or wyvern. (sculptural fragment installed on a wall of All Saints' Church), ca mid-tenth century (© Rev. Christ Tolley).

Fig. 5. Sinnington. Head and upper torso of a bear (fragment of a hogback monument), ca mid-tenth century (© Rev. Chris Tolley).

The remnant of a large hogback monument, probably removed from a Viking-age cemetery, juts from the base of the northeast exterior nave-wall, where it was installed during the twelfth-century rebuilding campaign (fig. 5).

This fragment is carved with a bear's head and upper body, now quite weathered. While most hogbacks have not survived intact, the themes of their various sculptural programs exhibit the same mélange of pre-Christian and Christian imagery appropriate to the cemeteries of those in cultural dialogue and religious flux.

The Bear and the Swan/Goose from Stonegrave

An interesting sculpture is also preserved at Stonegrave, North Yorkshire. It is a large fragment of a pre-Norman grave-lid/-marker (fig. 6). The side panel on this remnant displays a modified interlace pattern. The carving in the central panel features a bear-like beast, portrayed moving, while a goose/swan hovers over its back. J. Lang restricts his discussion of this monument to style-analysis, noting that it is "pronouncedly local, restricted to a single site, which not even the next village was tempted to copy" (Lang 1997, 73). This leads him to conclude that:

> The tenth-century group at Stonegrave in North Yorkshire is an example, standing out with complete distinctiveness from the Ryedale school pieces which surround it. Its fret patterns and iconography point westwards, not necessarily all the way to Ireland. This may well represent "estate sculpture" rather than anything approaching a local style, and it is consequently impossible to accommodate either stylistically or chronologically even in the Yorkshire series (Lang 1997, 73).[39]

Fig. 6. Stonegrave. Side panel of a fragment of a hogback with bear and goose/swan, ca mid-tenth century (© Rev. Chris Tolley).

A hand-written notice identifies "tentatively and fancifully" the image as "the Holy Spirit alighting on the Lamb of God".[40] Indeed, an examination of the carving

---

[39] See also Firby and Lang (1981, passim).
[40] The quotation is from communications with Rev. Tolley who found the notice with this inscription when he visited the church. Rev. Tolley has kindly permitted use of his photographs.

demonstrates that whoever identified the animals felt compelled to interpret them within Christian iconographic traditions. Yet, in this instance, it is meaningful to entertain alternative theories and investigate the possibility that this iconography also supports the contention that representations of pre-Christian beliefs entered the Christian sphere. Perhaps aware of the meaning of the swan/goose for the tenth-century *pagani*, early medieval clerics permitted these images, redefining them in Christian contexts. As discussed above, because of their habits and instinctive modes of behavior, the migrating goose/swan and the hibernating bear were perceived to be messengers between the earthly and divine realms and functioned as psychopomps. On this particular sculpture, the crosses are badly worn and barely visible. However, it seems likely that again, for a short time in pre-Norman Britain, the living sought to ensure safe passage for the deceased by uniting pre-Christian and Christian symbols in a Christian setting. Hogbacks adorned with muzzled bears can also be found at other sites in North Yorkshire including Brompton, where naturalistic bears are carved in high relief. Other hogbacks have been discovered in Scotland (Lang 1972-4, passim). At Brompton, and at other sites where the end-beasts are more stylized, the meaning(s) of the muzzled bears hugging each end of the monument probably evoked the same symbolic message of protection, and perhaps transportation, of the soul. In the period of re-Christianization, the presence of the muzzled bears would have comforted the *rustici* in their hopes that the souls entrusted to the graves would be kept safe and brought to their final destination of eternal rest.

The Boar and the Crucifixion Plaque from Penrith

Another interesting artifact that Richard Bailey discusses at length is a fragmentary, early-tenth-century Crucifixion plaque from Penrith, Cumbria (Bailey 1986, passim). On its reverse face is a hastily-etched image of a boar, the Celtic symbol of the priestly class. Bailey is of the opinion that this "graffito boar on the back is a later addition" and that "its meaning and stylistic relationships are not the least intriguing aspects of this fascinating piece but lie outside the scope of this paper" (ibid, 14). Yet, in this instance, this shallow carving of a boar, on the back of a Christian artifact depicting the Crucifixion, supports the contention that the sculptor who etched it had knowledge of pre-Christian beliefs and/or was instructed to depict the motif, probably by the patron. It also implies that whoever would see the boar (if, indeed, it could be seen) would have understood its significance.[41] As mentioned above, in pre-Christian Celtic belief, the boar was the symbol of the priestly class (Moreau 1995, 158; Thibaud 1995, 342-43). In the Christian Faith, Christ is the penultimate priest. Newly-converted Christians or re-Christianized *rustici* may have utilized the image of a boar as an apotropaic offering to their former gods and as a form of insurance against any retribution from an abandoned deity.[42] It may also have facilitated Christian instruction through use of familiar, pagan, motifs.

Thus far, Insular sculptural evidence has demonstrated that pre-Christian themes and symbols were utilized in Christian contexts. As Lang observed, the hogback funerary monument, depicting naturalistic or stylized bears, had a brief florescence. Are we then to surmise that beliefs in the old gods had completely disappeared once the bear and other animals, endowed with special meanings, disappeared from memorial art? On the contrary, can we find other traces of such beliefs in a different form and/or in a different context? As mentioned above, the bear and the wild/green man were conflated in the Middle Ages. Sculpted depictions of the wild man/green man, the "*feuillu*", are found in many churches, both in the British Isles and on the Continent (Basford 1978, passim). However, no longer are these later images the direct representation of particular ritualistic beliefs. They borrow from, and amalgamate, a vast repertoire of ancient cultural elements, yet their resultant "meanings" are abstracted and generalized. For example, the numerous examples of the "*feuillu*", or green man, suggest vague association with death, rebirth and/or demonic entities.

Early Medieval Continental Sculpture and Its Symbolism

By turning to the Continent, one can assess how similar pre-Christian beliefs evolved in a different Christian context. Such concepts were also depicted in Continental sculpture, demonstrating the legacy of pre-Christian beliefs and ritualistic practices in early medieval Europe (Muchembled 1985, 33). Perhaps because of cultural differences and sensibilities, the manner in which the Insular sculptor and his Continental counterparts chose to portray the rituals associated with Celtic, Germano-Scandinavian pre-Christian beliefs differed. Indeed, the Insular sculptors chose to emphasize the beginning of winter and the rituals associated with the feast of *Samane* (the keeping and protecting of souls by muzzled bears, and the psychopompic role of the bear and of the goose/swan, prior to the souls' return to life); whereas the Continental sculptor (see below) chose to display the ceremonial attires and rites associated with the feasts of *Imbolc* and *Beltane* (the apparent "resurrection" of the bear, and the ritualistic performances surrounding the release of souls and the greening of the earth in the spring).

---

[41] For a discussion of the function of the Crucifixion panel, see Bailey (1986, 14).

[42] According to Thibaud (1995, 342), "Manifestation de Lug, d'Esus et rival de Cernunos, doté d'une puissance peu commune, d'un temperament solitaire et combatif, le sanglier illustrait pour les celtes le pouvoir sacerdotal inaccessible au pouvoir royal".

The Bear and the Wild Man/Green Man from the Crypt at St Bénigne (Dijon)

The region of Burgundy is not only renowned for its medieval churches and sculptural programs, but also for its strong attachment to its Gallo-Celtic roots.[43] Before becoming the capital of Burgundy, Dijon (*Divio*) was a Gallo-Roman city, located not far from Bibract, the ancient capital of the Aeduen Celts.[44] Dijon is the site of the Basilica of St Bénigne, a third-century martyr. As the bishop of Langres, a city close to Dijon, the future Pope St Gregory the Great was suspicious of the cult devoted to St Bénigne, believing it was superstitious and demonstrated latent paganism. Perhaps in an effort to Christianize this cult and eliminate its "non-conformity", Bishop Gregory built a crypt (*ca* 511) designed for the veneration of St Bénigne's relics. The Merovingian church built over the crypt did not survive repeated Frankish and Moorish raids and fell into ruin. Shortly after the beginning of the second millennium, William of Volpiano rebuilt the church of St Bénigne. Today, the crypt is the only remaining part of William's church (Grodecki, 1986, 86-87). The dating of the sculpted capitals crowning the columns supporting the crypt is uncertain. They may have been part of a late ninth/early tenth century restoration of the original Merovingian Church, or part of William's rebuilding campaign.[45] Despite such chronological uncertainties, it is important to remember that the medieval crypt functioned as a place where the relics of saints were kept and were subjected to public veneration--often bordering on superstition.

Several sculpted capitals depict figural representations in various stages of completion. Two are remarkable because of their sculptural themes. Again, a bear-like creature makes its appearance on a capital of the rotunda (fig. 7).

This entity with ursine features seems to be lying on his back. He is surrounded by leaves and writhing creatures. He is holding his mouth wide open with paws that resemble human hands. His torso is striated, as though he were wearing some type of fury garment. He is showing the sole of his lower paws, and reveals his genitals and anus. This strange, perhaps esoteric, representation demands explanation. However, before investigating the possible symbolism attached to this particular sculpture, it is important to consider another on a different capital, as their iconographic programs seem to be linked.

Fig. 7. Crypt of the Basilica of St. Bénigne at Dijon. The awakening bear, ca tenth to early eleventh century (© N. Kleinsmith).

The most complete and striking examples of a "wild man/green man" are carved on the capital of a column flanking an altar located in an alcove of the crypt (fig. 8). On each side, the sculptor represents a standing man, with his arms outstretched in the position of an orant (figs. 8 and 8a). He wears ceremonial attire consisting of a long robe, belted at the hips, and a large cape and head-cover, both comprised of large palm leaves. His general appearance evokes that of a priest of some pre-Christian sect clad in ceremonial garments. While his features are recognizably human, they seem stiff and unnatural, as though the man wears a mask.

Despite differences in media, it is difficult to ignore the similarities with the human features on a Gallo-Roman ceremonial bronze helmet from Autun (fig. 9; especially the shape of the eyes and nose, and the vines or leaves which either cover or sprout from the mouths). The front of the helmet is surrounded by layers of bronze leaves attached to bands of leather that articulate the pieces around the wearer's neck and upper shoulders. It is hypothesized that this helmet functioned as a ceremonial head-covering (Pinette, Ganay, et al., 1987, 251-53). Given the helmet's approximate date of first century B.C., it is likely that these ceremonies were associated with the worship of pre-Christian deities. Since the helmet was originally gilded, it was probably worn by an important ritual-participant. The leaves, often associated with new growth, would have made the helmet an appropriate part of the ceremonial attire used during rituals associated with the rites of spring.

When considering the sculpted image of the bear, his posture, his open mouth and his anal orifice are reminders of the rites associated with the awakening of the bear at *Imbolc* and the release of souls at *Beltane*. Additionally, the inclusion of a depiction of a bear and his avatar, the wild/green man, in a crypt where saints' relics were kept,

---

[43] Bribact, the capital of the Celtic Aeduens is located on Mont Beuvron in Burgundy, not far from Autun, Saulieu and Dijon.
[44] In their attempt to destroy Aeduen powers, the new Romans built the city of *Augustodunum* (Autun) to replace Bibract. For more information on Celtic and pre-Romanesque Saulieu, see Moreau ([1763] 1889, passim).
[45] Basford (1978, Pl. 12) prefers a ninth-century date. Other researchers favor the eleventh century when William of Volpiano rebuilt the Church (begun 1001). See Grodecki (1986, 69); and Zarnecki (1979, 171-172).

Fig. 8. Crypt of the Basilica of St Bénigne at Dijon. Alcove with altar flanked by "L'Homme feuillu", ca tenth to early eleventh century (© N. Kleinsmith).

Fig. 9. Autun (France), Musée Rolin. Ceremonial helmet, ca first century B.C (© Musée Rolin).

Fig. 8a. Crypt of the Basilica of St. Bénigne at Dijon. "L'Homme feuillu", ca tenth to early eleventh century (© N. Kleinsmith).

implies a close association with bodily resurrection and with the return of life in the spring. Also, in Christian iconography, the palm leaves, which surround the green man at St Bénigne, are related to Christ's Resurrection. Indeed, these evergreen leaves are symbols of victory, regeneration, and immortality, and are often attributes of those who were martyred for their Faith (Quiñones 1995, 115-47, esp. 137; Chevalier and Gheerbrant 2000, 724). It seems that belief in the efficacy of such images, ensuring the return of life in the spring, was deeply anchored in the traditional beliefs of the inhabitants of Burgundy. By representing such iconography in the crypt, Christian clerics demonstrated that the pagan ritual had been subsumed and that pre-Christian beliefs had been absorbed into the fabric of the Church.

The "Pet de l'Ours" and the "Spring Festival" at Saulieu

Another example of such sculpted images may be found in Saulieu, a city even closer than Dijon to the ancient Celtic capital of Bibract. A church, dedicated to St Andoche, was built following a basilican plan ca 590-610.[46] This church did not survive the frequent Moorish

---

[46] According to Moreau ([1763] 1889, 3), referencing the seventh-century *Missale Gothicum*, the future St Polycarp, then Bishop of Smyrna, sent three devoted men, Andoche, Thyrse and Bénigne, to evangelize the local population. Martyred for their faith, the remains of these three second-century martyrs were deposited in a crypt where the

raids and internecine wars fought in the following centuries (Courtois 1984, passim). While the dating of Burgundian architecture and sculpture has been contentious throughout most of the twentieth century, recent research places the beginning of the reconstruction of the present church at *ca* 1080 (Theuret 1997, 3; Thibaud 1996, 16). The sculptures that are of interest here were carved on the capitals installed in the nave of the rebuilt church between 1080 and 1130.[47] St Andoche Basilica contains many sculpted capitals adorned with esoteric figural representations. Two of these are examined in this article: the "Pet de l'ours" (the bear's fart; figs. 10a, 10b) and the "Spring Festival" (fig. 11).

Fig. 10b. Salieu, Basilica of St. Andoche. Right side of the "Pet-de-l'Ours", ca 1080-1130 (© N. Kleinsmith).

Fig. 10a. Salieu, Basilica of St. Andoche. Right side of the "Pet-de-l'Ours", ca 1080-1130 (© N. Kleinsmith).

local Christians came to venerate them in secret. After the *Edict of Toleration* (AD 311) Saulieu became a pilgrimage center, which later attracted saintly bishops and even royalty.

[47] Differing opinions based primarily on stylistic analysis date the Saulieu sculptures between the 1080s and the 1130s. For early dating of St Andoche, see Aubert (1946, 89); Aubert (1966, 619); Deschamps (1925, 28); Porter (1920, 82); Porter (1966, I, 114-115); Theuret (1997, 3); Thibaud (1996, 1). For later dating of the Basilica of St Andoche, after St Lazare at Autun, see Crozet (1940, 126). Grivot and Zarnecki (1961, 175-76) consider the Saulieu sculptures derivative of Autun; Forsyth (1980, passim, esp. 91) and Forsyth (1981, passim, esp. 63) dates the basilica after 1135. For a summary of the Burgundian dating debate, see Armi (1983, passim).

Fig. 11. Salieu, Basilica of St. Andoche. Nave capital, ca 1080-1130 (© www.Art Roman.net).

On the left side of the nave, part of the engaged capital of the fourth column facing the western entrance is decorated with an unusual figural representation. Identification of the theme in the brief literature dedicated to the sculptural program at St Andoche varies from

Terret's "le combat de deux lions, que deux personnages armés de bâtons semblent vouloir exciter à la lutte", to Truchis' "montreurs d'ours".[48] While concurring with Truchis' assessment, Thibaud, the latest researcher on St Andoche, recognizes the symbolic significance of some of the themes represented on the capitals, acknowledging that they may have originated from pre-Christian roots (Thibaud 1996, 34-35, 59-60).

On the western side of this capital, two affronted ursine creatures stand on their hind legs. Behind each creature, a man is represented in the act of grabbing and lifting the creatures' tails, revealing their anuses. This unusual iconography—especially in the context of a church—requires explanation. The men lifting the tails of the ursine creatures or bears are performing a vital function, for they are helping the bears to release the souls that they had taken with them into the earth when they had gone into hibernation at the time of the feast of *Samane* (the feast of the dead; Gaignebet and Lajoux 1985, 261, 283-84). Additionally, the men (one brandishing a long stick topped with a large, round implement, the other holding a large stone) appear poised to strike the bears (possibly an allusion to the ancient rituals that may have involved the killing of the animal). The bear's annual "death" and apparent "resurrection" could be used profitably by clerics to explain Christ's death and resurrection in simple terms that even the *rustici* could understand.

Another associated representation is located on the right side of the center aisle, on the capital closest to the altar, also facing west, towards the entrance to the church (fig. 11). The iconography of this capital has always been puzzling. At times, it was dismissed as a purely decorative scene; at others, it was conveniently ignored. Once again, a few, mostly discounted, details of the capital seem to associate the scene with the representation of a Gallo-Celtic ritual involving the bear and his role in the unending cycle of life.

On this capital, the bear is portrayed at the very top, directly under the *tailloir*. Only his head and his front paws are visible, as though he were emerging from his den at the beginning of spring. At the base of the capital, a monstrous, leonine head is devouring new growth. Within the protective confines of a figure-eight, formed by leaves curving at the top and meeting right below the bear's head, a human blows a horn. Additionally, what appear to be two dancing goats are anxiously raising their heads towards the bear, and a dog is barking in the bear's direction.[49] If the intent was to awaken the bear from his hibernation, their joint efforts were successful because the bear is portrayed in a wakened state. In this case, the monstrous head devouring and/or disgorging green growth symbolizes time that has the power to devour or regurgitate all life according to an unending cycle, a belief favored in primitive agrarian societies (Gaignebet and Lajoux 1985, 73). The bear's function is to ensure that the chronophagic monster, like the *Artio* of the Gallo-Roman bronze statue, is kept at bay, and that time is not inverted or stopped, which would result in a series of disastrous occurrences (ibid., 79). The Celtic concept of time has been briefly examined above. As an addendum, it is sufficient to note that the Celts believed in two categories of time: human or earthly time and divine time. Connection between the two occurred only during brief periods of the year, which the Celts considered dangerous for the continued well-being of humanity (Guyonvarc'h and Le Roux, 1990, 156-164). The function of the bear as guardian of souls was investigated above. Additionally, owing to his cyclical appearance and disappearance, the bear acted symbolically as a stabilizing force that protected and ensured the continuity of life's seasonal cycles. While the impasse endures between the bear and the chronophagic monster, the man, his goats, and his dog, symbolizing the human and animal worlds, are protected within the figure-eight wreath of foliage, another symbol for the eternal cycles of life. In *De scripturis et scriptoribus sacris*, a twelfth-century cleric, Hugh of St Victor, wrote that eight represents "l'éternité après le changement du temps".[50] The "Pet de l'Ours" and the "Spring Festival" illustrate the importance that these primitive ritualistic practices surrounding the renewal of life still held for the medieval Celtic Aeduens. They demonstrate, again, that clerics manipulated pre-Christian and Christian symbolism to instruct the *rustici* using images and concepts that were already familiar to them.

Conclusion

Several conclusions may be drawn from the images discussed in this article. In the mid-tenth century, northern England witnessed a flourishing of sculpted animal representations that suggest mingling of pre-Christian and Christian traditions. A lapse in the Christian faith, when the local populace felt abandoned by their Church and by their Saints during repeated destructive Viking incursions and internecine conflicts, probably facilitated a re-emergence of pre-Christian beliefs and rituals. This survival/revival may have led to the production of hogback sculptures with ursine end-beasts.[51] The Insular sculptors chose to display the ritual associated with the feast of *Samane*, when the "muzzled" bear guards the souls during long months of hibernation,

---

[48] For the "lions being forced to engage in a fight", see Terret (1919, 24); for the "bears and their handlers", see Truchis (1908, 103-118, esp. 110). Terret's mistaken identification of the animals as "lions" may be due to Eastern influences that had dethroned the bear as king of the animals. It may also explain the ambiguity of some of the bears' features.
[49] Truchis (1908, 110) describes the capital as "un chevrier accompagnant avec l'ollifant la danse des chèvres et d'un chien, aux cris d'un hibou et sous le regard ahuri d'un bœuf". Terret (1919, 21) refers to the scene as "une curieuse scène historiée qui représente un pâtre qui joue de la trompe et fait danser deux chèvres ". Terret also identifies the bear at the top of the capital supporting the *tailloir* as a "ruminant". Finally, both admit they ignore the meaning of this scene.
[50] Miquel and Picard (1995, 200) quote from Hugh of St Victor, *De scripturis et scriptoribus sacris*, in Baron (1957, 124).
[51] It may also have led to the production of other sculptures with pre-Christian elements, which have not been examined in this article.

ensuring their safe conduct. That such sculpture had no progeny is only partially correct. While bear-carvings on funerary stones were not produced beyond the second half of the tenth century, other reminders of ancient, pre-Christian beliefs in the form of the bear's avatar (the wild man/green man, the "*feuillu*" or "*masque à feuille*") appeared, later caricaturized and/or demonized.

As well, some Burgundian sculptures of the late tenth through late eleventh/early twelfth centuries seem to imply a similar preoccupation with the promotion of pre-Christian themes in Christian environments. Despite a common interest in the bear and its symbolic meaning, the Burgundian sculptors elected to represent the rituals associated with the feasts of *Imbolc* and *Beltane* (the awakening of the bear, his release of the souls of the dead needed to replenish the earth and the greening process). Because the sculptures at St Bénigne and at St Andoche are probably from a later date, the sculptors also elected to represent not only bears but the first complete image in stone of a full size wild man/green man. In spite of the differences in style and mode of representation, it is apparent that in Insular and Continental cultures of the early medieval period, animals such as the boar, the goose/swan, and the bear and his avatars, the wild man/green man, maintained their symbolic pre-Christian roles. These animals, especially the bear and his avatars, safeguarded both human and animal souls in order to ensure the return of greenery and the return of life in the spring. That they were carved in durable material relates to the importance that they held as apotropaic shields against the feared, potential retributions from abandoned deities.

Benedictine monks, including the widely traveled Cluniacs and their followers, played an important role in the re-Christianization of the Latin West, in the reconstruction of religious buildings and in the restoration of the spirituality of the Church. The reforms that they and their followers instigated as well as their appropriation and adaptation of pagan feast days and ceremonial attire seem to indicate the willingness of the clergy to compromise. These clerics were very much part of their world. As such, they probably understood the practicality of utilizing images with pre-Christian meanings in Christian precincts in the process of instructing *rustici*. Did they guess that these images would eventually lose their intrinsic pre-Christian meanings? Did they suspect that they would be demonized, ridiculed and/or transformed into meaningless, decorative elements? Henri Polge explains how time affects and changes rituals and myths. Applying this model to the bear and his functions, Polge describes how a ritual theme developed as early as prehistoric times becomes desacralized over the years, is turned into a folkloric diversion, then adult entertainment, and finally is transformed into a childish toy or game.[52] At this stage, all the fear and reverence that the main actor in the ritual may have received at some point in the remote past has disappeared (Polge 1980, 257). With time, the identities of the bear, and of his avatars the wild man/green man, were blurred and soon became completely interchangeable. In the Late Middle Ages, the bear/wild man/green man was transformed into a minor demon, his actions warped and ridiculed. Yet, even then, he remained associated with the concept of life, since he served as Hellequin's helper in *charivaris*, which were skewed versions of former fertility rites.[53]

Acknowledgements

Isolated as only a medieval scholar can be in Southern California, I want to thank the people who have helped make this article possible by providing me with some background information on early medieval Insular sculpture and those who have allowed me the use of the photographs included in my article. Thus, I want to express my gratitude to Derek Craig (*Corpus of Anglo-Saxon Stone Sculpture*, University of Durham) for providing me with bibliographical information on the hogback sculptures. I am also very appreciative of Rev. Chris Tolley's permission to use his photographs of the various hogbacks. I want to acknowledge the Musée Rolin in Autun for allowing me to use a picture of their "casque de parade". I am also grateful to my husband, J.J. Kleinsmith for helping me take some of the photographs. Last but not least, I want to thank John Osborne, my mentor, and Michael Reed for their continued friendship across many miles.

Bibliography

Adhémar, J. 1996. *Influences antiques dans l'art du Moyen Age français*, Editions du C.T.H.S. (Paris)

Armi, E.C. 1983. *Masons and Sculptors in Romanesque Burgundy – The New Aesthetic of Cluny III*, Pennsylvania State University (University Park and London)

Aubert, M. 1930. *La Bourgogne, la sculpture* (Paris)

Aubert, M. 1966. *Romanesque Cathedrals and Abbeys of France*. C. Girdlestone (trans.), Nicholas Vane (London).

Bailey, R. 1978. "The Chronology of Viking-Age Sculpture in Northumbria." in J.T. Lang (ed.), *Anglo-Saxon and Viking Age Sculpture*, B.A.R. British Series 49 (Oxford): 173-85

Bailey, R. 1980. *Viking Age Sculpture in Northern England*, Collins (London)

---

[52] This evolution perfectly describes the fate of the bear, ultimately transformed into a Teddy Bear, and of the goose, which became the subject of a French game, the "jeu de l'oie".

[53] For a thorough analysis of the historical development of the Wild Horde and Hellequin, see esp. Schmitt (1994, 93-121).

Bailey, R. 1986. "A Crucifixion Plaque from Cumbria", in Higgitt, John (ed.), *Early Medieval Sculpture in Britain and Ireland*. B.A.R. British Series 152 (Oxford): 5-21

Bailey, R. 1996. *England's Earliest Sculptors*, Pontifical Institute of Mediaeval Studies (Toronto)

Bailey, R. 2000. "Scandinavian Myth on Viking-period Stone Sculpture in England". G. Barnes and R.M. Clunies (eds), *Proceedings of the 11th International S.A.G.A. Conference* (Sydney, Australia): 15-23

Barbier, G. 1979. "Commentaires sur les chapiteaux de Saulieu", *Association des amis du Vieux Saulieu*, 2: 8-11

Baron, R. 1957, *Science et sagesse chez Hugues de Saint-Victor* (Paris)

Basford, K. 1978. *The Green Man*, D.S. Brewer (Ipswich)

Becker U. 1994. *The Continuum Encyclopedia of Symbols*. L.W. Garmer (trans.), Continuum (New York)

Bernard de Clairvaux. *Apologia ad Willelmum*, in J.P. Migne, (1854) *Patrologia Latina* CLXXXII, cols 914-16

Bernheimer, R. 1952. *Wild Men in the Middle Ages – A Study in Art, Sentiment and Demonology.*, Harvard University Press (Cambridge)

Bolgiani, F. 1981. "Religione popolare", *Augustinianum* 3: 7-75

Boglioni, P. 1983. "la sopravivenze pagane nel medioevo", in P. Slater, P. et al (eds.) *Traditions in Contact and Change. Selected Proceedings of the XIVth Congress of the International Association for the History of Religions*, Wilfrid Laurier Press (Waterloo): 349-52

Bonvin, J. and Trilloux, P. 1992. *Eglise Romane Lieu d'énergie. Pour une géobiologie du Sacré*, Editions Dervy (Paris)

Brunner, B. 2007. *Bears, A Brief History*, Yale University Press (New Haven and London)

Brunaux, J.-L. 1996. *Les religions gauloises – Rituels celtiques de la Gaule indépendante*, Editions Errance (Paris)

Burtails, J.A. 1997. *Pour comprendre les monuments de la France*, Gérard Monfort (Paris)

Cahill, T. 1995. *How the Irish Saved Civilization. The Untold Story of Ireland's Heroic Role from the Fall of the Roman Empire to the Rise of Medieval Europe*, Doubleday (New York)

Camus, M.-Th. 1992. *Sculpture romane en Poitou*, Picard (Paris)

Carlet, J. 1858. "Notice sur l'église Saint-Andoche de Saulieu", *Mémoires de la Commission archéologique du département de la Côte d'Or* 5 (Dijon): 81-114

Cazenave, M. (ed.). 1996. *Encyclopédie des symboles*, Librairie générale française (Paris)

Charnasse, A. (de). 1909. "Origine des paroisses rurales dans le département de Saône-et-Loire", *Mémoires de la Société Éduenne*, 37 (Autun): 35 ff.

Chélini, J. 1997. *L'aube du Moyen Age – Naissance de la chrétienté occidentale*, Picard (Paris)

Chevalier, J. and Gheerbrant, A. 2000. *Dictionnaire des symboles, mythes, rêves, coutumes, gestes, formes, figures, couleurs, nombres*, Robert Laffont S.A. et Editions Jupiter (Paris)

Collingwood, W. G. 1908. *Scandinavian Britain* (London)

Collingwood, W. G. 1909a. "Anglian and Anglo-Danish Sculpture at York", *Yorkshire Archaeological Journal*, 10: 149-213

Conant, K. J. 1973. *Carolingian and Romanesque Architecture – 800 to 1200*, Penguin Books (London and New York)

Cook, W. R. and Herzman, R. B. 1983. *The Medieval World View*, Oxford University Press (New York and Oxford)

Courtois, J.-É. 1984. "Saulieu médiéval et le monastère de Saint-Andoche", *Association des Amis du Vieux Saulieu* 5: 3-16

Courtois, J.-É. 1982. "L'église Saint-Andoche de Saulieu et la légende de sa fondation par Charlemagne - Mélanges offerts à Réné Louis", *La chanson de Geste et le mythe carolingien.* 5 vols. Vol. 2: 1175-1198

Crozet, R. 1968. "Étude sur les consécrations pontificales", *Bulletin Monumental* 126 (Paris): 210-211

Davy, M.-M. 1977. *Initiation á la symbolique romane*, Flammarion (Paris).

Deschamps, P. 1925. "Étude de la Renaissance de la sculpture en France à l'époque romane", *Bulletin Monumental* (Paris): 5-28.

Dinter, P. (ed.). 1980. *Corpus consuetudinum monasticarum* 10 (Siegburg)

Dontenville, H. 1948. *La mythologie francaise*, Payot (Paris)

Dontenville, H. 1966. *La France mythologique* (Nancy, France)

Duboscq, G. et al. 1979. *La religion populaire,* Colloque international du Centre National de Recherche Scientifique, 1977, Editions du CNRS (Paris)

Duchaussoy, J. 1972. *Le bestiaire divin ou la symbolique des animaux,* Le Courrier du Livre (Paris)

Edsman, C. M. 1956. "The Story of the Bear Wife in Nordic Tradition", *Ethnos, 21*: 38-56.

Ensemble Paroissial de Saulieu. 1997. *Saulieu, basilique Saint-Andoche* (Dijon).

Evans, J. 1950. *Cluniac Art of the Romanesque Period,* Cambridge University Press (Cambridge)

Fabre, D. 1978. *Jean de l'Ours, analyse formelle et thématique d'un conte populaire* (Carcassonne)

Firby, M. and Lang, J. T. 1981. "The pre-Conquest Sculpture at Stonegrave", *Yorkshire Archeological Journal* 53: 17-29

Fisher, E. A. 1959. *An Introduction to Anglo-Saxon Architecture and Sculpture,* Faber and Faber (London)

Focillon, H. [1938] 1992. *Moyen Age Roman et Gothique,* Armand Colin (Paris)

Forsyth, I. H. 1980. "The Romanesque Portal of the Church of Saint-Andoche at Saulieu (Côte d'Or)", *Gesta* 19/ 2: 83-94
Forsyth, I. H. 1981. "L'âne parlant: The Ass of Balaam in Burgundian Romanesque Sculpture", *Gesta* 20: 59-65

Foy, F. A., O. F. M. (ed.). 1981. *Catholic Almanac* (Huntington, Indiana)

Gaignebet, C. and Lajoux, J.-D. 1985. *Art profane et religion populaire au moyen âge,* Presses Universitaires de France (Paris)

Geary, P. 1986. "Sacred Commodities: The Circulation of Medieval Relics", in Appadurai, A. (ed.), *The Social Life of Things. Commodities in Cultural Perspective,* Cambridge University Press (Cambridge & New York): 169-191.

Green, M. 1989. *Symbol and Image in Celtic Religious Art,* Routledge (London & New York)

Grabar, A. [1979] 1994. *Les voies de la création en iconographie chrétienne,* Flammarion (Paris)

Grivot D. (Chanoine) and Zarnecki G.. 1961. *Gislebertus Sculptor of Autun,* The Orion Press (Oxford)

Grodecki, L. 1986. *Le moyen age retrouvé,* Flammarion (Paris)

Guyonvarc'h, C.J. and Le Roux, F. 1990. *La civilisation celtique,* Éditions Ouest-France (Rennes)

Guyonvarc'h, C.J. and Le Roux, F. 1986. *Les Druides,* Éditions Ouest-France (Rennes)

Hani, J. 1990. *Le symbolisme du temple chrétien,* Guy Trédaniel (Paris)

Hearn, M. F. 1981. *Romanesque Sculpture,* Cornell University Press (Ithaca, NY)

Heitz, C. 1987. *La France pré-romane,* Éditions Errance (Paris)

Henderson, E. F. (ed. and trans,). 1965. "The Rule of St. Benedict", *Select Historical Documents of the Middle Ages,* Prentice-Hall (Englewood Cliffs): 274-314

Hopper, V. F. 1995. *La symbolique médiévale des nombres,* Crevier, R. (trans.), Gérard Monfort (Paris)

Hückel, A. G. 1901. "Les poèmes satiriques d'Adalbéron", *Mélanges d'histoire du Moyen Age,* 13: 138-40

Husband, T. 1980. *The Wild Man. Medieval Myth and Symbolism,* Metropolitan Museum of Art (New York)

Iogna-Prat, D. 1998. *Ordonner et exclure – Cluny et la socété chrétienne face à l'hérésie, au judaisme et à l'islam, 1000-1150,* Aubier (Paris)

Jacq, C. 1980. *Le message des constructeurs de cathédrales,* Editions du Rocher (Paris)

James, L. 1996. "'Pray Not to Fall Into Temptation and Be on Your Guard': Pagan Statues in Christian Constantinople", *Gesta 36*/1: 12-20

Johnson, P. 1985. *A History of the English People,* Harper and Row (New York).

Jones, A. 1995. *Les saints,* Bordas (Paris)

Karkov, C. E., Farrell, R. T., Ryan, M. (eds.) 1997. *The Insular Tradition,* State University of New York Press (Albany)

Karkov, C. E. and Orton, F. 2003. *Theorizing Anglo-Saxon Stone Sculpture,* West Virginia University Press (Morgantown)

Kieckhefer, R. 1989. *Magic in the Middle Ages,* Cambridge University Press (Cambridge).

Klayman, M. [1997] 2002. "The Anglo-Scandinavian Hogback: a Tool for Assimilation", Pdf. File. 12 pages.

Lady Raglan. 1939. "The Green Man in Church Architecture", *Folklore* 50(1): 45-57

Lajoux, D. 1996. *L'homme et l'ours,* Éditions Glénat (Grenoble)

Laliberté, M. 2000. "Religion populaire et superstition au Moyen Age", *Théologiques* 8/1: 19-36

Lang, J. T. 1972-4. "Hogback Monuments in Scotland", *Proceedings of the Society of Antiq. Scot.,* CV, 206-235

Lang, J. T. 1978. "Anglo-Scandinavian Sculpture in Yorkshire", in Hall, R.A. (ed.), *Viking Age York and the North,* Council of British Archeology Research Report, 27 (London): 11-20

Lang, J. T. 1984. "The Hogback: A Viking Colonial Monument", *Anglo-Saxon Studies in Archaeology and History,* 3 (Oxford) 85-176

Lang, J.T. 1991. *Corpus of Anglo-Saxon Stone Sculpture, Vol. 3: York and Eastern Yorkshire,* Oxford U Press (Oxford)

Lang, J. T. 1997. "Survival and Revival in Insular Art, Some Principles", in Karkov, C. E., Farrell, R. T., Ryan, M. (eds.), *The Insular Tradition,* State University of New York Press (Albany): 63-78

Lang, J. T. 2002. *Corpus of Anglo-Saxon Stone Sculpture, Vol. 6: Northern Yorkshire,* Oxford U Press (Oxford)

Lauwers, M. 1990. "Religion populaire", in *Catholicisme. Hier, aujourd'hui et demain,* vol. 12. Letouzey et Ané (Paris): 835-49

Lecouteux, C. 1993. *Les monstres dans la pensée médiévale européenne,* Presses de l'Université de Paris-Sorbonne (Paris)

Le Jan, R. 1996. *Histoire de la France : Origines et premier essor 480 – 1180,* Hachette Supérieur (Paris)

Le Roux, F. and Guyonvarc'h, C.-J. 1995. *Les fêtes celtiques,* Éditions Ouest-France (Rennes)

Le Roux, F. and Guyonvarc'h, Ch-J. 1991. *La Société celtique,* Édilarge, Éditions Ouest-France (Rennes)

Little, L. K. and Rosenwein., B. H., (eds.) 1998. *Debating the Middle Ages: Issues and Readings,* Blackwell Publishers (Malden, MA and Oxford)

MacKillop, J. 2004. *Oxford Dictionary of Celtic Mythology,* Oxford University Press (Oxford)

McLynn, F. 1999. *1066, The Year of the Three Battles,* Pimlico (London)

Mango, C. 1984. *Byzantium and its Image,* Valorium Reprints (London)

Mercier, P. (ed.). 1970. *XIX Homélies du IXe siècle,* Le Cerf, Sources chrétiennes (Paris)

Meslin, M. 1984. *Le merveilleux, l'imaginaire et les croyances in Occident,* Bordas (Paris)

Miquel, P, O.P. 1992. *Dictionnaire symbolique des animaux,* Le Léopard d'Or (Paris)

Miquel, P., O.P. and Picard, P. O.S.B. 1995. *Dictionnaire des symboles liturgique,* Le Léopard d'Or (Paris)

Moreau, M. 1995. *La Tradition celtique,* Le Courrier du livre (Paris)

Moreau, P. (Canon and Cantor). 1763. "Notes sur Saulieu et principalement sur l'église de Saint-Andoche", (Dijon), in Ferrand, F.-E (ed.). 1889. *L'église Saint-Andoche d'après les manuscrits inédits* (Dijon)

Moore, R.I. 1977. *The Origins of European Dissent.* Allen Lane (London)

Moore, R.I. 1987. *The Formation of a Persecuting Society: Power and Deviance in Western Europe,* Blackwell (Oxford)

Muchembled, R. 1985. *Popular Culture and Elite Culture in France,* Cochrane, L. (trans.), Louisiana State University Press (Baton Rouge & London)

Oursel, Ch. 1928. *L'art roman de Bourgogne, études d'histoire et d'archéologie.* (Dijon et Boston)

Oursel, R. 1968. *Bourgogne romane,* La nuit des temps 1. Zodiaque (Vauban-Saint-Léger)

Pacaut, M. 1994. *L'ordre de Cluny,* Fayard (Paris)
Pastoureau, M. 2007. *L'Ours, histoire d'un roi déchu,* Seuil (Paris)

Pastoureau, M. 2002. *Les animaux célèbres,* Bonneton (Paris)

Patoureau, M. 1985. "Quel est le roi des animaux?" in *Le monde animal et ses représentations au Moyen Age* (Toulouse) : 133-142

Pastoureau, M. 1988. "Ours, lion, aigle: enquête sur le roi des animaux", *L'Histoire* 114: 16-24

Pennick, N. 1997. *The Sacred World of the Celts, An Illustrated guide to Celtic Spirituality and Mytholog,* Inner Traditions International (Rochester, Vermont)

Petzold, A. 1995. *Romanesque Art,* Harry N. Abrams (New York)

Pietri, L. 1988. "Les origines de la fête de la Toussaint", *Les Quatre fleuves,* 25-61

Pinette, M., Ganay, S. (de), et al (eds.) 1987. *Autun – Augustodunum, Capitale des Eduens. Catalogue de l'exposition du 16 mars au 27 octobre 1985,* Imprimerie Pelux (Autun)

Plongeron, B. (ed.) 1976. *La religion populaire, approches historiques,* Beauchesne (Paris)

Polge, H. 1980. "Jeux et divertissements ou de l'enfance à la préhistoire", *Mélanges de mythologie francaise* (Paris)

Porter, A. K. 1920. "La sculpture du XIIe siècle en Bourgogne", *Gazette des Beaux Arts* 62 (Paris): 74-94

Porter, A. K. 1966. *Romanesque Sculpture of the Pilgrimage Road,.* 10 vols, Hacker Art Books (New York): Vol 1

Praneuf, M. 1989. *L'homme et l'ours dans les traditions européennes* (Paris)

Quiñones, A. M.. 1995. *Symboles végétaux – La flore sculptée dans l'art médiéval,* Desclée de Brouwer (Paris)

Rudolph, C. 1990. *The "Things of Greater Importance": Bernard of Clairvaux's Apologia and the Medieval Attitude Towards Art,* University of Pennsylvania Press (Philadelphia)

Saintyves, P, Desforges, A and Guignard-Nourry, L.. 1998. *Pierres à légendes de Bourgogne,* Les Éditions du Pas de l'Âne (Dijon)

Sawyer, P.H. 1978. "Some Sources for the History of Viking Northumbria", in R.A. Hall (ed.), *Viking Age York and the north,* Council of British Archeology Research Report, 27 (London): 8-10

Schmitt, J.-C. 1988. "Les 'superstitions'", Le Goff, J. and Rémond, R. (eds.), *Histoire de la France religieuse.* Vol. 1, *Des Dieux de la Gaule à la papauté d'Avigon* (Paris).

Schmitt, J.-C. 1994. *Ghosts in the Middle Ages – The Living and the Dead in Medieval Society,* F. T. Lavender (trans.), University of Chicago Press (Chicago and London)

Schmitt, J.-C. 1998. "Religion, Folklore, and Society in the Medieval West", in L. K. Little and B. H. Rosenwein (eds.), *Debating the Middle Ages: Issues and Readings,* Part IV, "Religion and Society", Blackwell Publishers (Malden, MA and Oxford): 376-87

Schnürer, G. 1935. *L'église et la civilisation au moyen age* (Paris)

Seringe, P. 1995. *Les symboles dans l'art, dans les religions et dans la vie de tous les jours,* Éditions Hélios (Genève)

Shapiro, M. 1979. *Late Antique, Early Christian and Mediaeval Art,* George Braziller (New York)

Smyth, A. P. 1978. "The Chronology of Northumbrian history in the ninth and tenth centuries", in R.A. Hall (ed.), *Viking Age York and the north,* Council of British Archeology Research Report, 27 (London): 3-7

Soufflet, P. 1981. "Continental Influences on English Romanesque Sculpture", *Oxford Art Journal* 4/2 (Oxford): 5-9

Stone, L. [1955] 1972. *Sculpture in Britain: The Middle Ages,* Penguin Books (Middlesex)

Stratford, N. 1998. *Studies in Burgundian Romanesque Sculpture,* 2 vols, Pindar Press (London)

Sumpton, J. 1975. *Pilgrimage: An Image of Mediaeval Religion,* Faber and Faber (London)

Terret, V. 1919. *Saulieu et la collégiale Saint-Andoche,* Dejussieu et Xavier (Autun)

Terrillon G. et J.–P. 1977. "Basilique Saint-Andoche", *Saulieu en Morvan* (Saulieu): 18-35

Theuret, A. 1997. *La basilique Saint Andoche de Saulieu* (Dijon)

Thibaud, R.-J. 1995. *Dictionnaire de mythologie et de symbolique celte,* Éditions Dervy (Paris)

Thibaud, R.-J. 1996. *Saulieu, berceau de l'ésotérisme chrétien,* L'Arbre de Jessé (Joigny, France)

Thornton, T.C.G. 1986. "The Destruction of Idols – Sinful or Meritorious?" *Journal of Theological Studies,* 37: 121-129

Truchis, P. (de). 1908. "L'église Saint-Andoche de Saulieu", *Congrès archéologique 74. Avallon, 1907* (Paris): 103-118

Van Gennep, A. 1947. *Manuel du folklore français contemporain,* 3 vols, vol. 1 Picard (Paris): 833-1416

Voisenet, J. 1994. *Bestiaire chrétien – l'imagerie animale des auteurs du haut moyen- âge (Ve – XIe siècle),* Presses universitaires du Mirail (Toulouse)

Voisenet, J. 2000. *Bêtes et Hommes dans le monde médiéval,* Brépols Publishers (Turnhout, Belgium)

Walsh, M. J. (ed.) 1998. *Butler's Life of the Saints* (Cambridge & New York)

Walsh, M. J. 1998. *Lives of the Popes,* Barnes & Noble (New York)

Whitelock. D. 1955. *English Historical Documents, 1, c. 500-1042* (New York)

Wittkower, R. 1942. "Marvels of the East. A study in the History of Monsters", *Journal of the Warburg and Courtauld Institutes* 5 (London): 159-197

Zarnecki, G. 1979. "Romanesque Sculpture in Normandy and England in the Eleventh Century", in R. A. Brown (ed.), *Proceedings of the Battle Conference 1978,* The Boydell Press (Ipswich): 168-189

Zarnecki, G. 1986. "Sculpture in Stone in the English Romanesque Art Exhibition", in S. Macready and F.H. Thompson (eds), *Art and Patronage in the English Romanesque,* The Society of Antiquaries of London (London): 7-27

Putting Memory in its Place:
Sculpture, Cemetery Topography and Commemoration

Zoë L. Devlin, Ph.D.
University of York

The study of the stone sculpture of tenth- and eleventh-century England was once largely the preserve of art historians who focused on the artistic and didactic qualities of the surviving pieces and their origins (e.g. Bailey 1978; 1980; 1996; Cramp 1984; 1992; Hawkes 2002; Karkov and Orton 2003; see Reed in this volume; and Reed 2009 for the history of the study of stone sculpture). In more recent years, however, Anglo-Saxon stone sculpture has attracted the attention of archaeologists interested in the construction and maintenance of identity. Scholars such as Stocker (2000), Everson (Stocker and Everson 2001), Sidebottom (2000) and Hadley (2002), among others, have argued that the commission of stone sculpture to mark the burial places of the dead was one way in which the elite made statements about their social status, ethnic background, gender and religious beliefs. These studies have done a great deal to highlight the ways in which stone sculpture played an active part in people's social identity and made statements about similarity and difference within and between communities. However, such archaeological interpretations are focused primarily on the needs and concerns of the living. In contrast, the commemorative aspects of the sculpture, which were presumably the most important consideration for the people at the time, have been much neglected by scholars.

Cemeteries as Places

Developments within post-processualist schools of thought within archaeology have encouraged the study of people's experiences and understandings of the environment in which they lived (Ashmore and Knapp (eds.) 1999; Barrett 1994; Bender 1993; Howe and Wolfe 2002; Ingold 1993; 2000; Tilley 1994; 2004). Such studies have drawn upon perspectives from philosophy, anthropology and sociology to consider the impact that specific places might have had on people's lives (e.g. Boyarin 1994; Casey 1996; Craik 1986; Hirsch and O'Hanlon 1995; Tuan 1979). These perspectives have shown that the environment in which people live is not a passive backdrop to events of the past. Instead, landscape and place are active in shaping people's lives, their activities, their experiences and their opportunities. The ways in which people understand and perceive a particular place are directly related to their experiences of it and this, in turn, is related to their position within society, with certain places being restricted to people of a particular social status and others being openly accessible. The result is that the meaning of a place is derived from the contemporary social and cultural context and can change over time. Time is an important variable in understanding place as it is repeated activity in a place over time that gives that place its meaning. Memory is inherently related to understandings of place as it allows people to relate current events there to existing perceptions and earlier actions (Chesson 2001; Jonker 1995; Kujit 2001). The place itself, therefore, and its physical environment are crucial in defining the kinds of activities that go on there and the ways in which those activities are understood by the people who participate in them.

Cemeteries can be seen as special places. They are subject to different time cycles and are the scene of repeated ritualised activities that occur outside the realm of 'normal', everyday life (Barley 1995; see also Devlin 2007, 49, 74). The cemetery can be understood as being outside normal time, creating links between the past and the present through the ties between the living and the dead and projecting the memory of the dead forward into the future. The act of burying the dead and the funerary rites that accompany it have only a temporary significance for commemoration (Hadley 2001; Halsall 1998; 2003). However, the grave itself can serve as a focus for continuing memorial activity, perhaps for generations to come (Williams 2006). Several studies have already indicated the importance of the experience of place in the siting of early medieval cemeteries (e.g. Brookes 2007; Carver 2002; Lucy 1998; Roymans 1995; Williams 1999). However, the topography of the cemetery itself can also be seen to be crucial for the shaping of people's experiences within it and for the remembrance of the dead (Devlin 2007, 43-80). The emergence of stone grave markers in the later Anglo-Saxon period indicates a change in the approaches to commemorating the dead on the part of some families. However, such grave markers were a part of much wider activities aimed at remembering the dead that took place within the cemetery (for discussions of later Anglo-Saxon burial rites in general and of the variety of grave markers in particular, see Devlin 2007, 49-58, especially 55-57; Hadley 2001, especially 125-140; Hadley and Buckberry 2005, especially 140-143; Williams 2006). To understand the commemorative aspects of stone sculpture therefore we must put it back into its original context. Although it is rare to find stone sculpture *in situ* over a grave, sufficient evidence survives from some sites for us to gain a strong understanding of how contemporaries might have seen it. This paper will focus on two sites where this was the case: the graveyards from St Mark's church, Lincoln, and Raunds Furnells, Northamptonshire.

St Mark's, Lincoln

Excavations took place within the modern churchyard of St Mark's, Lincoln, in 1976 following the demolition of the church prior to development on the site. The site had served as a burial ground for roughly one thousand years and unravelling the stratigraphy of many of the features on the site has been problematic. A recent review of the stratigraphy of the whole of the site (Steane 2001, especially 279-280) has led to a reinterpretation of the development of the late Anglo-Saxon cemetery, with some of Gilmour and Stocker's (1986) initial interpretations being reconsidered. In particular, the argument that the first phase of Anglo-Saxon burials (Gilmour and Stocker's Period VIII) was accompanied by a wooden post-built church to the south-east and was bounded by a ditch and substantial timber fence to the west has been abandoned, and some of the burials have been rephrased.[1] The cemetery was located in the newly developed suburb of Wigford to the south of Lincoln, in an area that had been occupied during the Roman period but had subsequently been abandoned when the area of settlement contracted. The cemetery lay to the west of Ermine Street, which served as its eastern boundary and presumably acted as the main point of access. The excavated area was not large enough to uncover the whole of the cemetery, and it is clear that burial continued outside the limits of the excavation. The area of land given over for burial was naturally restricted to the west by the river, although in the first phase of the cemetery's use burial did not reach this far, being demarcated instead by a ridge of high ground in the middle of the site (Gilmour and Stocker 1986, 15). Similarly, Ermine Street provided a boundary to the east, while the extent of the cemetery to the north and south was probably limited by neighbouring properties. There is no direct archaeological evidence that the cemetery at St Mark's was surrounded by a specially created boundary marker, such as a wall, fence or ditch. The creation of such a boundary marker at an Anglo-Saxon cemetery site tends only to occur with the construction of a church and the attendant need to define the sacred space around it (Devlin 2007, 57-58; Gittos 2002). If there was no church in this first phase of the cemetery's use, it is also likely there was no boundary marker. On the other hand, the alignment of the graves might indicate a boundary feature did exist, even if we have no direct evidence archaeologically. Although the graves are laid out on a roughly west-east alignment, this is not a true west-east alignment; rather they are laid out perpendicular to the road. As Anglo-Saxon burials tend to be laid out in relation to an existing physical or geographical feature (Devlin 2007, 49-51, 55), it seems likely either that a wall, ditch or fence did exist to the north and/or south of the site, or that a church was constructed in an area where any archaeological trace of it has been lost. Such a boundary marker or building would then have served as a feature on which to align the graves.

Radiocarbon dating and sculptural evidence indicates that burial began in the mid-tenth century (Gilmour and Stocker 1986, 16-17; Steane 2001, 253, 279). Burial from this first phase of the cemetery's use was quite crowded (see fig. 1). Despite the lack of a physical boundary marker there seems to have been some restriction against burial extending into the open ground to the west, perhaps because of the risk of flooding from the river as suggested by Gilmour and Stocker (1986, 90), or perhaps because any burial there would be less visible from the rest of the cemetery due to the way the land sloped down to the river. Burial on the higher ground was therefore considered more desirable. It can be expected that the cemetery would have been even more crowded by the end of the first phase than it appears on the site plan. Many graves may have been destroyed by subsequent burials and the construction of later church buildings. The apparent clustering of burials into large groups on the site plan (fig. 1) is therefore largely the result of later activity rather than deliberate planning, with the foundations of the walls of the first stone church in particular removing many burials (cf. fig. 2). However, there does seem to have been a tendency to place certain graves close together. Many near-contemporary graves overlap each other without causing damage to the earlier burial and it is possible that they were deliberately placed close together in order to create associations between the graves. Men, women and children are found fairly evenly distributed across all areas of the cemetery, although there is a slight tendency for women to be buried in the southern part of the excavated area rather than elsewhere. This distribution, along with the clustering of graves into small groups, implies that burial was organised in family plots.

In the mid-eleventh century, roughly one hundred years after its foundation, there was a massive reorganisation of the cemetery (Gilmour and Stocker 1986, 17-19). A stone church was founded that cut across earlier burials, burying some under the church floor and destroying others altogether (see fig. 2). The church also cut across the edge of high ground above the river beyond which no phase 1 burials had been located. Burial extended into this area of marginal land at this time although few burials can be attributed to this phase, with people preferring to bury their dead in established areas to the north and south of the new church. In this second phase of the cemetery (Gilmour and Stocker's Period IX), the orientation of graves remains the same as in the earlier phase but is also clearly associated with the position and orientation of the stone church. Although the distribution of male, female and child burials implies a preference towards burying women and children to the north of the

---

[1] The 'church' is now associated with the Roman settlement phase and the fence with an internal structure in the later medieval church (Steane 2001).

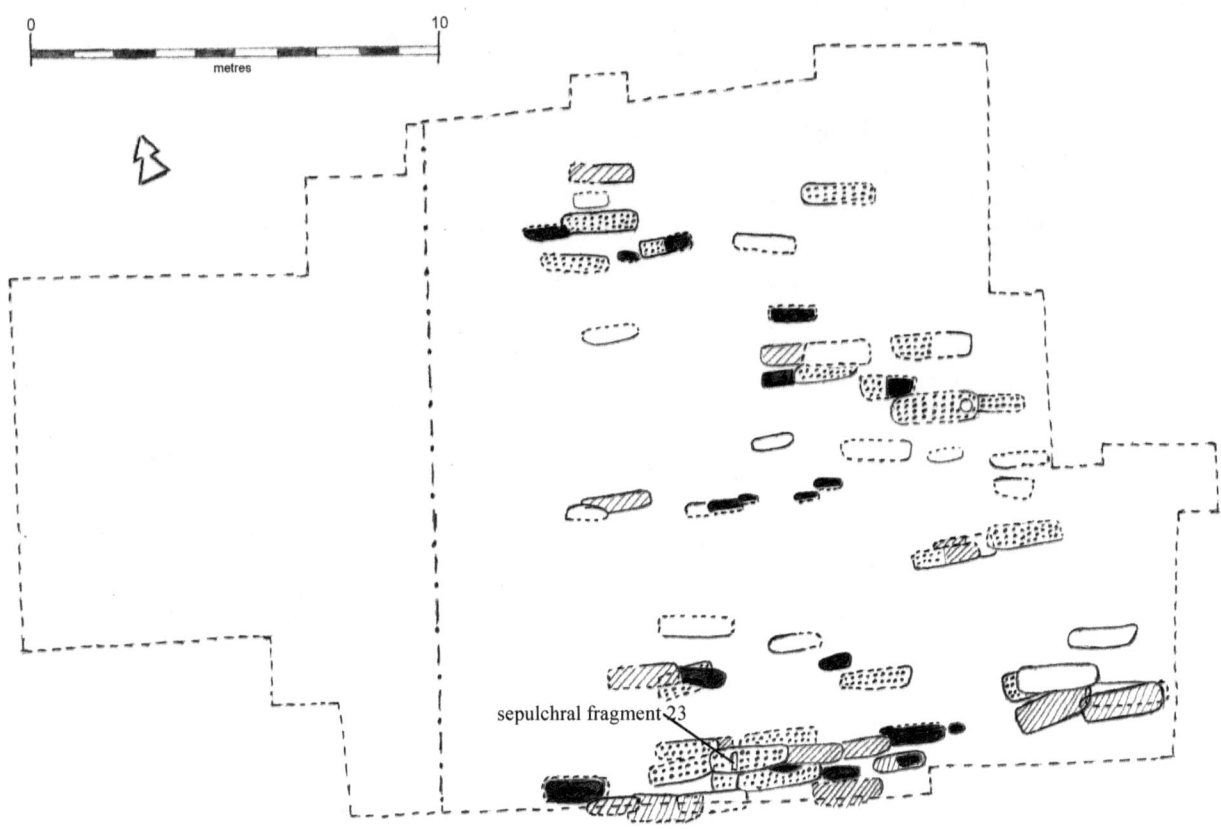

Fig. 1. St Mark's, first phase, showing men (stippled), women (diagonal lines) and children (black) (redrawn by the author after Gilmour and Stocker 1986). The vertical broken line indicates the edge of the high ground.

church in this phase, the family plots of the earlier phase seem to have continued in use (fig. 2). Burial in these plots should therefore be considered as a single sequence that spans the time before and after the church was built, rather than as the two distinct phases that the site plans suggest.

Around fourteen fragmentary stone grave markers are attributable to the first two phases of burial at St Mark's, datable to the period between the mid-tenth and later eleventh centuries. Four more can only be dated to between the mid-tenth and thirteenth centuries, so may also possibly be from this phase. Only one of these was found *in situ*, sepulchral fragment 23, which was found above the grave of a man aged 25-35 years when he died (Gilmour and Stocker 1986, 63-64). The remainder were all found reused in the foundations of the later medieval church (early thirteenth-century) or in the fabric of the Victorian building, found during restoration in the nineteenth century (Everson and Stocker 1999; Gilmour and Stocker 1986). The unusually high number and the overall quality of the grave markers recovered from the site have led David Stocker *et al.* to argue that St Mark's was the burial site of several high status families, albeit some apparently more wealthy than others (Gilmour and Stocker 1986, 91; Stocker 2000; Stocker and Everson 2001). Remembrance of the dead was closely linked to their visibility. Although all forms of grave marker would

have made particular graves more visible to passers-by, stone memorials would have made the burial place even more noticeable. Their size, permanence, bright colours and known expense made them ideal mnemonic devices, extending the remembrance of the dead person beyond their immediate family and friends to the rest of the community. This would have been of great importance at a time when remembrance was equated with prayers for the soul's salvation. The living could directly help the souls of the dead through their prayers; the more people remembering the dead and feeling obligated towards them, the more prayers would be said for their soul. At least ten of the Anglo-Saxon grave markers discovered in the foundations of the medieval church were cross-shaped or had a cross decoration carved onto them. Sepulchral fragment 23, found *in situ*, was also an upright cross. Such decoration would have acted as a constant reminder of salvation and the future resurrection on the Day of Judgement and therefore of the need to pray for the soul.

The use of stone sculpture would have advertised the deceased's status within the community. As well as acting as a mnemonic for prayers for the dead person, the high status implied by the stone sculpture acted as a reminder of the importance of the deceased in the community and hence of the ties and obligations felt towards them by others within that community. The longevity of stone grave markers also meant that

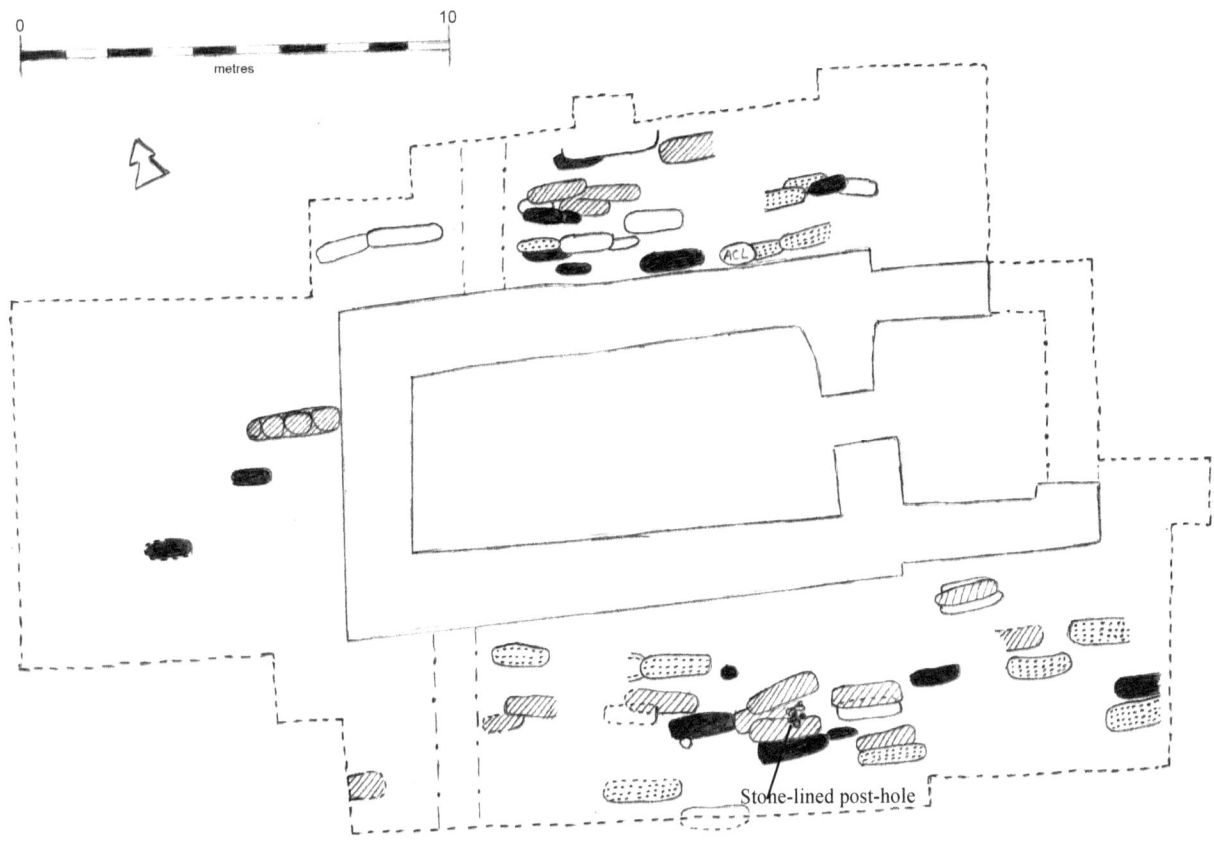

Fig. 2. St Mark's, second phase, showing men (stippled), women (diagonal lines) and children (black) (redrawn by the author after Gilmour and Stocker 1986). The broken vertical lines indicate possible paths to the church.

potentially these obligations were not limited to people who knew the deceased personally but might also be expected of future generations.

The ways in which people moved around the cemetery would also have been of importance for the remembrance of the dead, as burials that were close to paths would have been more prominent and those buried there more likely to be remembered in prayers. It is notable that in both phases under discussion here there seems to have been a marked propensity to bury the dead close to the road and therefore near to the cemetery's point of access. There is little evidence for any other form of grave marker being used at St Mark's, although it is likely each grave was covered by a small mound. The only other evidence for grave markers was a stone-lined wooden post-hole between graves 377 and 378.[2] This may have marked grave 375 beneath it and the alignments of the two subsequent burials 377 and 378 seem to respect it. The stone markers and any other wooden marker posts would have stood out prominently in the graveyard, drawing the eye to the graves they marked. The thirteen sepulchral fragments that survived to be used in the foundations of the later medieval church presumably represent just a few examples of the grave markers that were actually in use during the tenth and eleventh centuries. Their use in the foundations of the later medieval rebuilding of the nave suggests that they stood in the graveyard for around 150-200 years, an observation supported by the degree of weathering on them (Gilmour and Stocker 1986, 63). It could be argued that for them to survive for so long when other examples presumably did not they must have been marking the graves of people who were remembered for some time after their death, most likely because their family remained in the area and were active and important members of the community, ensuring the memories of their ancestors, to whom they owed their social position, were commemorated in the church. On the other hand, these grave markers may have been re-used several times during their lifetime to mark different graves. What is clear though is that by the early thirteenth century the knowledge of who was buried beneath them would have been long forgotten, allowing them to be used as building material.

The building of the stone church in the second phase of the cemetery's use represents a major disjuncture with the remembrance of the dead in the earlier phase. The church was built on top of a large number of burials, destroying many. It is unclear exactly what happened to the remains disturbed in this area; it is assumed that they were redeposited somewhere within the cemetery, perhaps

---

[2] The post-holes that were originally thought to be related to wooden marker posts associated with Period IX burials have since been reinterpreted as Roman features (Steane 2001).

becoming indistinguishable from later medieval interments (Gilmour and Stocker 1986). It might also be expected that the construction of the stone church led to pathways being re-routed around the cemetery, whether the church building was an entirely new foundation or whether there had been an earlier church on the site. There is little evidence for the existence of pathways in the first phase of burial although doubtless there were well-worn routes from the road to different parts of the cemetery. These paths may well have changed and developed organically over time as more burials were added and the topography of the cemetery changed. The building of the stone church led to the creation of new paths that centred on the building. These may well have been planned, rather than developing organically, along with the siting of the church itself. Although no archaeological evidence was found for external doorways, the distribution of graves outside suggests there were paths leading to entrances in the west end of the north and south walls of the nave (fig. 2). These paths presumably connected with others that led to the boundaries. An existing route-way has been suggested to the north in the vicinity of the modern St Mark's Street (Gilmour and Stocker 1986) although each cemetery path may have connected to Ermine Street to the east. The existence of pathways would have enhanced the desirability of those locations for burial, as graves would have been more visible and it is notable that to the north of the church in particular there was a cluster of burials beside the projected path.

At St Mark's the family seems to have been particularly important for the way the dead were remembered. The family would still have been central to dealing with the dead, organising the funeral and taking a prominent role in remembrance activities, despite the increasing involvement of the clergy at this time (Devlin 2007, 79-80). The dead were interred in family plots and each individual would have been remembered in relation to their place in the family. Each funeral would have revived memories of previous burials and would have served as an opportunity to talk about other family members and their deaths. The use of stone grave markers over particular graves would have served to mark the whole plot, not just the grave over which it was placed. In this way the purchase of such an expensive piece of grave furniture was an investment for the whole family and their souls. The building of the stone church seems to have caused a massive disruption in the remembrance practices of certain families, with some graves being apparently moved or destroyed to make way for the foundations and others being sealed by the floor of the church itself so that they could no longer be accessed or visited by mourners. It might be that these graves belonged to families who were no longer living in the area or who did not have the influence to gainsay the location of the church. The breaking up and re-use of many grave markers in the fabric of the church might suggest the former explanation rather than the latter as it is likely that at least some of those markers came from graves that were affected by the construction and a family who could afford stone sculpture might be expected to have some power and influence. Alternatively, the survival of a cluster of graves from the earlier phase under the chancel might indicate another explanation. These burials ended up being very close to the altar in the church, a highly desirable location. The site and position of the church might have been chosen deliberately to cover the graves of the founder's family. In addition, if the stone church was an entirely new foundation it would have completely altered the way that commemoration was carried out on the site. If there was no church on the site when burial first began commemorative rituals must have been carried out at another church, away from the grave and the bodies of the dead. Presumably, other separate rituals would then have been carried out at the graveside. With the construction of a church, this changed and the commemorative rituals would have been able to incorporate the physical location of the grave much more fluidly into the remembrance services, perhaps through processions around the graveyard and into the church. The church itself would therefore also have become a focus for remembrance, incorporating other rituals that were important milestones in people's lives such as baptisms and marriages, which were important sources for memories.

Raunds Furnells, Northamptonshire

The church at Raunds Furnells in Northamptonshire provides a contrast to that at St Mark's, Lincoln, but also highlights the similarities in commemorative practices between different communities in the later Anglo-Saxon period. St Mark's represents an urban community in a growing mercantile town. The unusually large numbers of stone grave markers reflect the prosperity of the community that used the church there. Raunds, in contrast, represents a smaller, rural community. The church was founded in the late ninth or early tenth century as a single-celled stone building and was associated with a manorial complex close by, to the west of the church (Boddington 1996, 5). In the mid-tenth century, the church building was extended by the addition of a chancel and burial began at the same time (ibid., 5-6, 8, 11, 19-22, 67). The churchyard was clearly demarcated with a physical boundary in the form of a series of ditches surrounding the site, dug prior to the start of burial, and possibly with an internal bank (ibid., 14, 49). It is likely that this creation of a physical boundary was related to the consecration of the churchyard prior to the start of burial and was therefore associated with the construction of the chancel, rather than the initial church-building project (Gittos 2002). In the late eleventh to mid-twelfth century, the church was demolished and replaced with a larger building (Boddington 1996, 5, 8, 10). As with the construction of the church at St Mark's, Lincoln, this caused disruption to the wider cemetery, with some burials being destroyed and others being disinterred and reburied elsewhere (ibid., 10).

The use of the Raunds churchyard for burial was relatively short-lived, with new burial ceasing shortly

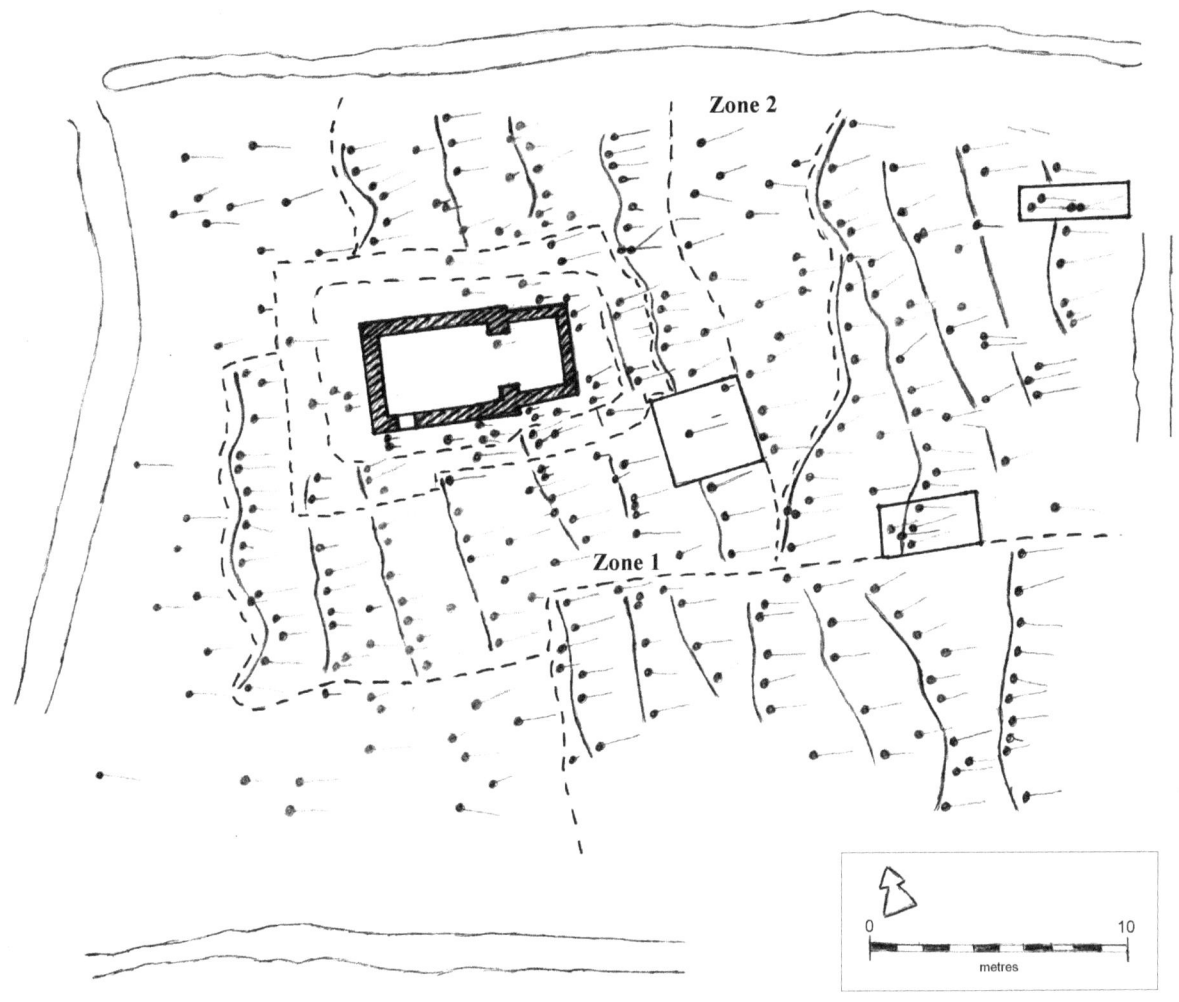

Fig. 3. Andy Boddington's interpretation of Raunds Furnells showing zones, rows and plots (redrawn by the author, based on Boddington 1996).

after the rebuilding of the church. Burial was on a true west-east orientation, with the church building acting as the dominant means of orienting the graves. Most of the graves match the alignment of the church, with the exception of a few outlying burials which are aligned on the boundary ditch close by. Physical features of the cemetery were therefore the defining aspect of burial orientation; however, it is likely that a liturgical west-east orientation was intended for the graves at Raunds. The boundary ditches themselves were on slightly different alignment to the church, lying on the same orientation as the pre-existing manorial site (Boddington 1996, 10). Although there is little in the way of vertical stratigraphy, most of the burials seem to be associated with the first church building (ibid., 13). There is clear evidence that the layout of the cemetery was carefully planned, with graves being placed in rows stretching from north to south. Burial started to the south of the church before spreading in zones to the west and then to the east, with 'infilling' of any gaps and the addition of 'eaves-drip' child burials immediately adjacent to the church walls towards the end of the burial period (ibid., 6, 11-12, 53-57; see fig. 3). The existence of these rows implies there was someone in overall authority, dictating how the cemetery could be used. Unlike St Mark's, Lincoln, where families seem to have been buried together, the newly deceased at Raunds were added to the end of an existing row rather than being placed with other family members. This control does seem to partly break down at one stage however, with the beginning of burial in Zone 2 to the east of the church being less regimented than other areas and with the apparent insertion of later burials in-between existing ones in some rows. Some graves disturbed existing burials (Boddington 1996, 27-28), but it is unclear whether this was the result of an attempt to place individuals near to relatives or whether the existence of the original grave had been forgotten. However, as a rule there is little evidence for the burial of the dead in family plots at Raunds. The only apparent exceptions to this are two plots (marked as rectangles on fig. 3) that contained four and five burials, respectively. Burial close to the church building was clearly considered the most desirable, with the insertion of burials into the space between the church walls and the earliest burials in Zone 1 rather than spreading to the edges of the cemetery where there was ample space. The existence of eaves-drip child and infant burials is mirrored at other sites of this period (e.g. Cherry Hinton, Buckinghamshire) and is thought to reflect a concern for children to have 'eternal baptism' through the rainwater running off from the church roof. There is some evidence for gendered division of burial location, with males in Zone 1 concentrated south of the church while more females than males were displaced to the edges of the cemetery as burial in the zones became more crowded (Boddington 1996, 55).

Raunds is a rare example of a cemetery site where several stone grave markers have been found *in situ*. These include: two graves with carved stone covers, one of which was probably re-used from another context; six more covered with one or more rough stones; seven with rough stones at the head and/or foot of the grave; and one marked by a stone cross. Fragments from two more stone crosses and one decorated slab were found in the fabric of the second church or that of the later medieval manorial house built on the same site but could not be matched with a particular grave (Cramp 1996, 103-7). In addition, at least seven graves were marked by a wooden post or cross at the head or foot of the grave and two groups of graves were marked by a long slot that may have been the foundation of a fence. Altogether the excavator suggests around 36 graves had some form of special marker out of a total recovered population of 363 people (Boddington 1996, 45-46; five coffins may also have had covers at ground level). The most important of these marked graves was that of a man aged 35-45 buried to the south-east of the church, apparently in a plot of his own, covered with a stone grave cover decorated with interlace and marked by a large stone cross, apparently of matching design. This grave has been interpreted as a 'founder's grave' by Andy Boddington (1996, 11, 51, 67) and seems to have affected the layout of the cemetery throughout its use, with the surrounding area being largely respected by all the other burials. This individual might be supposed to have been the owner of the nearby manor house and, if not the founder of the church, a member of their family. There is a strong contrast here with the use of stone grave markers at St Mark's, which represents the commemorative practices of several families, rather than the single elite family with access to such markers at Raunds. It is possible that the other forms of grave markers belong to relatively high status members of the community close to Raunds, imitating the lordly family living at the manor and using stone sculpture to mark the graves of their families. However, we must not assume that such practices would have been of concern only to the more wealthy members of a society and undressed stone and wooden posts would presumably have been accessible to all.

There does seem to have been far more control by a single authority over the placing of graves at Raunds than at St Mark's, with stricter adherence to rows and less intercutting. This might also imply that the choosing of grave markers, and who was entitled to have the graves marked, would also have been tightly controlled. The fact that the majority of people buried at Raunds, and at other cemeteries in this period, did not have archaeologically visible markers seems to imply either that this form of marking graves was a strictly controlled practice across all churches or that this was a concern only of a relatively small number of people in society. While it might be the case that everyone in late Anglo-Saxon society was concerned about the fate of their soul, only a few could have the expectation of being remembered and prayed for by the whole community.

Access to and around the cemetery may have been less clearly defined at Raunds than at St Mark's, with little evidence of paths, except for a burial-free area immediately in front of the door in the south wall of the church. There is also little evidence for how the churchyard would have been accessed from outside. The manorial complex was to the west of the churchyard and there was a road accessing the manor to the north but there is no indication that there was a special entrance crossing the ditches. This lack of evidence for control over access and movement within the cemetery might suggest that while the layout was carefully controlled, the practice of commemorative activities might have been less so. Family memory may also have been less important at Raunds as, although there is evidence for some family plots within the rows, the development and spread of the cemetery implies that these plots were not maintained over long periods but instead that new rows were started. Maintenance of family memory through burying the dead together would only have been possible in the short term. As with St Mark's, the rebuilding of the church created issues for the continuing remembrance of the dead. Although there was less disruption to the site as a whole at Raunds, the building of the second church resulted in the destruction of some burials and the movement of others. The mounds and other markers close to the church were also cleared before the second programme of construction. In addition, the building of the second church was soon followed by the cessation of burial, which presumably moved elsewhere. It is unclear how long commemoration of the dead might have continued at Raunds after this, although the fact that the stone cross marking the founder's grave had made its way in to the foundations of the second church seems to imply that the memories associated with some areas of the site at least were already lost by this time.

Conclusion

The late Anglo-Saxon cemetery was not a passive recipient of the remains of the dead but had a crucial role to play in their ongoing remembrance. The topography and layout of the cemetery, the placing of the dead in relation to it and the methods of marking the grave were ways of structuring remembrance. The way the cemetery was organised had a direct affect on how areas within it could be accessed, which in turn would impact upon the effectiveness of commemorative rituals carried out there. The marking of graves, whether by small mounds or large pieces of stone sculpture, would have had the effect of channelling people along certain routes as well as highlighting the presence of the dead and drawing attention to them. The maintenance of such markers over time was a means by which the family preserved the memory of the deceased for the rest of the community. Failure to maintain the grave site led to the forgetting of the dead, with the erosion of earth mounds and the theft or collapse of free-standing markers. The degree of inter-cutting and over-laying of graves at sites such as St Mark's seem to indicate a burial generation of around 30 years, during which time most graves become indistinct and the person buried there was forgotten. The existence of stone grave markers seems to extend this period of the preservation of the grave – and with it the deceased's memory. It is likely that at both St Mark's and Raunds the carved markers remained *in situ* for between 100 and 200 years. Such markers not only served to call attention to the grave by making it more visible but acted as a powerful mnemonic for those individuals rich and powerful enough to afford such a marker. In doing so, such markers did not work alone but were incorporated into stories, gossip and rituals that remained a part of the life of the community for many years to come. The spread of stone grave markers in the tenth and eleventh centuries can be seen as one part of a number of changes to the way the dead and their memory were treated in the later Anglo-Saxon period. With the development of ideas regarding the importance of the prayers of the living for the salvation of the dead, remembrance took on a whole new aspect, with the fate of the soul depending upon the projection of individual memory into the future. The commissioning of stone sculpture by the laity therefore represents one aspect of the fight against oblivion in which all aspects of cemetery topography played a part.

Acknowledgements

I would like to thank the participants at the New Voices on Early Medieval Sculpture conference, 2007, especially David Stocker, for their comments on this paper. A version of this paper was also presented at the Department of Archaeology Research Seminar, Cardiff University, in April 2008, where it received many helpful comments from colleagues and research students. Any errors remain my own.

Bibliography

Ashmore, W. and Knapp, A.B. (eds.) 1999. *Archaeologies of Landscape. Contemporary Perspectives*, Blackwell Publishers (Massachusetts and London)

Bailey, R. 1978. 'The chronology of Viking Age sculpture in Northumbria', in J. Lang (ed.), *Anglo-Saxon and Viking Age Sculpture and its Context: Papers from the Collingwood Symposium on Insular Sculpture from 800-1066*, B.A.R., Brit. Ser., 49 (Oxford): 173-203

Bailey, R. 1980. *Viking Age Sculpture in Northern England*, Collins (London)

Bailey, R. 1996. *England's Earliest Sculptors*, Pontifical Institute of Medieval Studies (Toronto)

Barley, N. 1995. *Dancing on the Grave. Encounters with Death*, John Murray (Publishers) Ltd (London)

Barrett, J.C. 1994. *Fragments From Antiquity. An Archaeology of Social Life in Britain, 2900-1200 BC*, Blackwell Publishers (Oxford)

Bender, B. (ed.) 1993. *Landscape. Politics and Perspectives*, Berg (Providence & Oxford)

Boddington, A. 1996. *Raunds Furnells. The Anglo-Saxon Church and Churchyard*, English Heritage Archaeological Report, 7 (London)

Boyarin, J. 1994. 'Space, time and the politics of memory', in J. Boyarin (ed.), *Remapping Memory. The Politics of TimeSpace*, University of Minnesota Press (Minneapolis and London): 1-37

Brookes, S. 2007. 'Walking with Anglo-Saxons: landscapes of the dead in early Anglo-Saxon Kent', in S. Semple and H. Williams (eds.), *Anglo-Saxon Studies in Archaeology and History*, 14: 143-153

Carver, M.O.H. 2002. 'Reflections on the meanings of monumental barrows in Anglo-Saxon England', in S. Lucy & A. Reynolds (eds.), *Burial in Early Medieval England and Wales*, The Society for Medieval Archaeology (London): 132-141

Casey, E.S. 1996. 'How to get from space to place in a fairly short stretch of time', in S. Feld and K.H. Basso (eds.), *Senses of Place*, School of American Research Press (Santa Fe): 13-32

Chesson, M.S. 2001. 'Embodied memories of place and people: death and society in an early urban community', in M.S. Chesson (ed.), *Social Memory, Identity and Death: Anthropological Perspectives on Mortuary Rituals*, Archaeological Papers of the American Anthropological Association, 10 (Naperville, Illinois): 100-113

Craik, K.H. 1986. 'Psychological reflections on landscape', in E.C. Penning-Rowsell and D. Lowenthal (eds.), *Landscape Meanings and Values*, Allen and Unwin (Publishers) Ltd (London): 48-64

Cramp, R. 1984. *Grammar of Anglo-Saxon Ornament*, Oxford University Press (Oxford)

Cramp, R. 1992. *Studies in Anglo-Saxon Sculpture*, Pindar Press (London)

Cramp, R. 1996. 'The monumental stone', in A. Boddington, *Raunds Furnells. The Anglo-Saxon Church and Churchyard*, English Heritage Archaeological Report, 7 (London): 102-112

Devlin, Z. 2007. *Remembering the Dead in Anglo-Saxon England: Memory Theory in Archaeology and History*, B.A.R., Brit. Ser., 446 (Oxford)

Everson, P. and Stocker, D. 1999. *Corpus of Anglo-Saxon Stone Sculpture. Volume V. Lincolnshire*, Oxford University Press for the British Academy (Oxford)

Gilmour, B.J.J. and Stocker, D.A. 1986. *St Mark's Church and Cemetery*, Council for British Archaeology (London)

Gittos, H. 2002. 'Creating the sacred: Anglo-Saxon rites for consecrating cemeteries', in S. Lucy and A. Reynolds (eds.), *Burial in Early Medieval England and Wales*, Society for Medieval Archaeology (London): 195-208

Hadley, D.M. 2001. *Death in Medieval England. An Archaeology*, Tempus Publishing Ltd (Stroud)

Hadley, D.M. 2002. 'Burial practices in northern England in the late Anglo-Saxon period', in S. Lucy and A. Reynolds (eds.), *Burial in Early Medieval England and Wales*, Society for Medieval Archaeology (London): 209-228

Hadley, D.M. and Buckberry, J. 2005. 'Caring for the dead in late Anglo-Saxon England', in F. Tinti (ed.), *Pastoral Care in Late Anglo-Saxon England*, Boydell and Brewer (Woodbridge): 121-147

Halsall, G. 1998. 'Burial, ritual and Merovingian society', in J. Hill and M. Swan (eds.), *The Community, the Family and the Saint. Patterns of Power in Early Medieval Europe*, Selected Proceedings of the International Medieval Congress, University of Leeds, 1994 and 1995, Brepols (Turnhout): 325-338

Halsall, G. 2003. 'Burial writes: graves, "texts" and time in early Merovingian northern Gaul', in J. Jarnut and M. Wemhoff (eds.), *Erinnerungskultur im Bestattungsritual. Archäologisch-Historisches Forum*, Wilhelm Fink Verlag (Munich): 61-74

Hawkes, J. 2002. *The Sandbach Crosses: Sign and Significance in Anglo-Saxon Sculpture*, Four Courts Press (Dublin)

Hirsch, E. and O'Hanlon, M. 1995. *The Anthropology of Landscape. Perspectives on Place and Space*, Oxford University Press (Oxford and New York)

Howe, J. and Wolfe, M. (eds.) 2002. *Inventing Medieval Landscapes. Senses of Place in Western Europe*, University of Florida Press (Gainesville, FL)

Ingold, T. 1993. 'The temporality of the landscape', *World Archaeology*, 25 (2): 152-174

Ingold, T. 2000. *The Perception of the Environment. Essays in Livelihood, Dwelling and Skill*, Routledge (London and New York)

Jonker, G. 1995. *The Topography of Remembrance. The Dead, Tradition and Collective Memory in Mesopotamia*, Studies in the History of Religions Series, 68, E.J. Brill (Leiden, New York and Köln)

Karkov, C. and Orton, F. (eds.) 2003. *Theorizing Anglo-Saxon Stone Sculpture*, West Virginia University Press (Morgantown)

Kujit, I. 2001. 'Place, death and the transmission of social memory in early agricultural communities of the Near Eastern Pre-Pottery Neolithic', in M.S. Chesson (ed.), *Social Memory, Identity and Death: Anthropological Perspectives on Mortuary Rituals*, Archaeological Papers of the American Anthropological Association, 10 (Naperville, Illinois): 80-99

Lucy, S. 1998. *The Early Anglo-Saxon Cemeteries of East Yorkshire. An Analysis and Reinterpretation*, British Archaeological Reports, British series, 272 (Oxford)

Reed, M.F. 2009. 'Sculpture and lordship in Late Saxon Suffolk: the evidence of Ixworth', in Z.L. Devlin and C.N.J. Holas-Clark (eds.), *Approaching Interdisciplinarity: Using History and Archaeology together for the study of early medieval Britain, c.400-1100*, B.A.R., Brit. Ser., 486 (Oxford)

Roymans, N. 1995. 'The cultural biography of urnfields and the long-term history of a mythical Landscape', *Archaeological Dialogues*, 2: 2-38

Sidebottom, P. 2000. 'Viking Age stone monuments and social identity in Derbyshire', in D.M. Hadley and J.D. Richards (eds.), *Cultures in Contact: Scandinavian Settlement in England in the Ninth and Tenth Centuries*, Brepols (Turnhout): 213-235

Steane, K. 2001. *The Archaeology of Wigford and the Brayford Pool*, Oxbow Books (Oxford)

Stocker, D. 2000. 'Monuments and merchants: irregularities in the distribution of stone sculpture in Lincolnshire and Yorkshire in the tenth century', in D.M. Hadley and J.D. Richards (eds.), *Cultures in Contact: Scandinavian Settlement in England in the Ninth and Tenth Centuries*, Brepols (Turnhout): 179-212

Stocker, D. and Everson, P. 2001. 'Five towns funerals: decoding diversity in Danelaw stone sculpture', in J. Graham-Campbell, R. Hall, J. Jesch and D.N. Parsons (eds.), *Vikings in the Danelaw*, Oxbow (Oxford): 223-243

Tilley, C. 1994. *A Phenomenology of Landscape. Places, Paths and Monuments*, Berg (Oxford)

Tilley, C. 2004. *The Materiality of Stone. Explorations in Landscape Phenomenology*, Berg (Oxford & New York)

Tuan, Y.-F. 1979. 'Thought and landscape. The eye and the mind's eye', in D. Meinig (ed.), *The Interpretation of Ordinary Landscapes*, Oxford University Press (Oxford)

Williams, H. 1999. 'Placing the dead: investigating the location of wealthy barrow burials in seventh century England', in M. Rundkvist (ed.), *Grave Matters. Eight Studies of First Millennium AD Burials in Crimea, England and Southern Scandinavia*, B.A.R., Int. Ser., 781 (Oxford): 57-86

Williams, H. 2006. *Death and Memory in Early Medieval Britain*, Cambridge University Press (Cambridge)

A Cross-head from St Mary Castlegate, York, and its Affiliations

Victoria Whitworth, Ph.D.
Independent Scholar, Orkney

A fragmentary cross-head from St Mary Castlegate, York, raises some interesting questions about the ecclesiastical culture of tenth-century Northumbria. While this stone, and the others from the site, have received a degree of scholarly attention, the cultural implications they raise have not hitherto been explored in any great detail.

St Mary Castlegate: Background

St Mary Castlegate is one of a cluster of churches in York founded before the Norman Conquest with associated tenth- or eleventh- century sculpture. The church stands in the immediate vicinity of the excavated tenth- to eleventh-century site at 16-22 Coppergate: it was clearly in a densely-inhabited area of the city. There is some extant eleventh-century masonry in the nave (St Mary's Church, Castlegate, York 2006). The recorded sculptural assemblage at St Mary's consists of nine stones, two of which have been lost. One of the extant stones (7 in the *Corpus of Anglo-Saxon Stone Sculpture* numbering, Lang 1991) carries an inscription in Latin and Old English recording the building of the church and its dedication to Christ, St Mary and All Saints by patrons with Scandinavian names (Higgitt in Lang 1991). There are two recumbent grave-covers (5 and 6), one of which (5) is coped and elaborate, and the remains of four crosses. The coped grave-cover and one of the cross-heads (2) have strikingly close affiliations with two pieces of sculpture from Sinnington, N. Yorks, fifty kilometres away. Except for another of the cross-heads (see below), all the extant sculpture is carved in sandstone.

St Mary Castlegate: Cross-Head 3

The exception is cross-head 3, carved from a soft, fine, pale limestone. Like the other sculpture, it very probably represents the re-use of worked stone from Roman Eburacum (Lang 1991). It survives in three pieces, one of which was found during nineteenth-century restoration work and the other two (which carry traces of plaster and paint) during twentieth-century excavation (Tweddle in Wenham *et al.* 1987). There have been several attempts at reconstruction (Collingwood 1927, Hall 1975, Tweddle in Wenham *et al.* 1987), which differ in minor details. All, however, agree that this was once a ring-headed cross, with on one face an elaborate series of bosses and, on the other, four crouching animals, one on each arm.

The ends of the arms of the cross protrude beyond the ring and are decorated with a plate and boss. Lang uses the word 'unique' twice in his discussion of this cross, once to describe the plate-and-boss ends, and once to describe the crouching animals, which he refers to as 'canine animals' and 'dogs' (Lang 1991). Tweddle refers more cautiously to a 'crouched quadruped' and 'crouched animals'; like Lang's, his discussion is concerned with date and ethnic affiliation, and stylistic and formal connexions (Tweddle in Wenham *et al.* 1987). Both come to the same broad conclusions: that the cross is tenth-century, Anglo-Scandinavian, and very unusual. Collingwood, who had only one fragment to study, raised the tentative possibility that images on the four arms of the cross might have represented the four Evangelists, and that the 'little beast, modelled in the round' might be 'the Lion of St Mark'. (Collingwood 1909, 1927): this would imply the calf, lion and man of the other evangelists on the other arms. However he was clearly dissatisfied with this hypothesis, and in his reconstruction drawing he chose to show an animal on each arm, as later proved to be the case (Collingwood 1927). Collingwood's rejected hypothesis remains the only previous suggestion as to the meaning of this stone's iconography.

St Mary Castlegate 3: the Animals

Three animals survive on the extant arms of the cross, one complete but for its head and one fore-paw. The others are hacked back to little more than scars on the stone, but from what can be seen they look as though they are intended to be identical and it is plausible, with Collingwood, to guess that the missing fourth arm was also carved with an animal. A composite analysis of the three surviving carvings suggests a creature with rounded haunches, a tail that curves straight up to lie flat along the spine, stylised hind legs and naturalistic, well-defined, splayed front paws. Collingwood's reconstruction suggests a raised head, presumably because there is no obvious scar on the stone where a head has been chipped away. The heads and the front paws of the beasts would have intruded into the central space of the cross, very close to any boss marking the crossing.

Previous scholarship thus offers two lines of enquiry: that these are dogs (Lang) or lions (Collingwood), and claims that they are unique. These creatures are indeed unparalleled in Anglo-Saxon sculpture: however, there is

Fig. 1. St Mary Castlegate 3: the face with the three dogs/lions. Image courtesy of the Corpus of Anglo-Saxon Stone Sculpture, University of Durham. Photographer: Tom Middlemass.

a series of striking parallels from Ireland and the west of Scotland. In a study unrelated to St Mary Castlegate, Hawkes has explored the significance of some of these in her assessment of a cross-head from Mayo Abbey, co. Mayo, Ireland (Hawkes, 2001). This is a free-armed cross-head of Anglian type which Hawkes dates to the late eighth- to early ninth-century; she identifies the figure on one face as the risen Christ and draws attention to an animal crouching on the top of the upper cross-arm, which she identifies firmly as a lion, although it is extremely badly weathered. She adduces mid-eighth-century parallels from Iona (two confronted creatures on the top of the upper cross-arm on the Cross of St John, also very weathered, and broken) and Kildalton (four creatures set around the central boss). At Kildalton, the crouched creatures above and below the boss are shown from above, and here the resemblance to St Mary Castlegate is striking. Hawkes, drawing on patristic writings, reads the lion, at Mayo and elsewhere, as a symbol of the resurrected Christ, and she draws attention to connexions between Mayo, Iona, and Northumbria, especially York. Evidence for the connexions between Mayo and York fades out before the tenth century, although in c.800 it was under the jurisdiction of the Archbishop of York (Hughes in Clemoes and Hughes, 1971).

However, Hawkes does not suggest a reason why there should be multiple images of lions at Iona and Kildalton; nor does she discuss a group of Irish monuments which also have crouched animals carved as though seen from above but disposed very differently about their crosses.

Three sites in Ireland and Northern Ireland (Drumcliff, co. Sligo; Donaghmore, co. Tyrone, Galloon, co. Fermanagh) produce four crosses with crouched beasts; Harbison categorises these as belonging to the Ulster group, and suggests a ninth-century date (Harbison, 1992). At Drumcliff, there are three beasts: one on the north end of the lateral cross arm and two on the underside of the ring, flanking the lower arm of the cross. Harbison distinguishes here between 'a lion in high relief' at the top of the shaft and the 'animal in high relief, facing downwards', immediately above it (Harbison, 1992), which suggests that he does not think the latter is obviously a lion. At Donaghmore there is a creature on each end of the lateral arm of the cross. At Galloon, where only the cross-shafts survive *in situ*, the animals creep down the south face of the East Cross and the north face of the West Cross. The Irish examples of these animals occur in a variety of iconographical contexts, but always on either or both the north or south face of the crosses, never the east or west, i.e. the main faces. They are always depicted from above, crouched. With the possible exception of the West Cross at Galloon, they do not appear in close proximity to human figures (and even here the animal does not form part of the scene with the possible figures). While Harbison only refers to them as animals a little more precision can be attained. There is no apparent stylisation or abstraction in the design. The animals have paws rather than hooves, there are no horns, they have short muzzles and small ears. No tail is visible. At Drumcliff (by far the best-preserved) they have well-modelled haunches. In other words, they are very like the creatures at St Mary Castlegate, more so than the animals at Iona, Kildalton or Mayo. At Drumcliff, Donaghmore and Galloon the animals are not given the prominence that they are at Iona, Kildalton and Mayo. They creep down the cross, always head-down, in comparatively obscure positions. At all three of these sites there is a creature to both north and south, although at Galloon they are on separate crosses. It is harder to read these animals as symbols of the triumphantly risen Lord. What then might they be? If not lions, is there any justification, given Lang's suggestion for the St Mary Castlegate cross, for the idea that they are dogs?

The many references to dogs in Scripture are overwhelmingly negative. Menache explores the general hostility of monotheistic religions to dogs: she suggests that dogs are inherently liminal creatures, often living on intimate terms with humankind and straddling the boundary between human and non-human, sacred and profane, and she points out that dogs are the only animal which St John associates with the whoremongers, sorcerers, murderers, idolaters and liars excluded from the kingdom of heaven, in Revelation 15:22 (Menache, 1997). In the context we are examining here, namely crosses, the most relevant biblical reference to dogs is 'For dogs have surrounded me; a gang of evildoers has closed in on me; they pierced my hands and my feet' from Psalm 21:17 (in the Vulgate numbering). This psalm is among the most prominent of the Old Testament texts interpreted as prophesies of the crucifixion, one that would have been known by heart by all members of a monastic or collegiate community through constant repetition. Its opening line, "My God, My God, why has thou forsaken me," was quoted by Christ on the cross, and St Augustine interprets the whole psalm as though spoken by Christ: an intensely personal dramatic monologue commenting on the experience of the Crucifixion (Hebgin and Corrigan, 1960). The psalm's encompassing dogs/evil-doers would make sense in terms of the disposition of the animals around the cross-head both at Donaghmore and Drumcliff, and at St Mary Castlegate; less so at Galloon unless we read both crosses together as part of a single monumental landscape: plausible, given that the two Galloon cross-shafts are so similar.

Whether dogs or lions, these creatures imply a complex interpretation of Christian belief that eschews the literal and the obvious: how is this developed by setting it in the context of the cross as a whole?

St Mary Castlegate 3: the Bosses

The other face of the St Mary Castlegate cross-head is as elaborate, and almost as unusual, as the face with the animals. The centre and the arms of the cross are each marked by a domed and decorated boss, against a background of cable and beading. The central boss is quite deeply carved, but some of the ornament on the others is quite lightly incised and may have been further picked out with paint. Lang draws attention to the Borre style origins of the motif on the central boss, and Tweddle suggests parallels that would place the cross in 'the late 9th century, or the first half of the 10th century' (Lang, 1991; Tweddle, 1987).

A cross-head with five highly-ornamented bosses is surely intended to invoke the five wounds of Christ. The obvious comparandum is 'The Dream of the Rood,' ll. 7b-9a, with its description of a cross with five jewels at the intersection. The cross the poem depicts is the *crux gemmata*, the jewelled cross with five gems representing the five wounds that will appear in the sky at the Second Coming, a staple of devotional art from at least the fifth century and well-known in Anglo-Saxon sculpture (Bailey, 1996). The subject of the Cross in the art and literature of Anglo-Saxon England and her neighbours has been studied exhaustively and there is no room here to cover again such well-trodden ground in any detail. Where stone crosses are concerned, there are parallels at Iona, among other places, for five bosses adorning the cross-head; and Bailey draws attention to the cluster of five bosses on the pre-Viking Age crosses at Irton (Cumbria) and Northallerton (N. Yorks) as representations of the five wounds (Bailey 1980 and 1996). The ornamented bosses at St Mary Castlegate thus assimilate images of the Crucifixion and the Second Coming in a way very familiar from much early medieval art and literature: to take but one literary example of many, Wulfstan, Archbishop of York, describes in one homily how at the Last Judgement Christ will display His wounds and ask what humankind has done for Him (Raw, 1990). It is only at the Second Coming that the true meaning of the Crucifixion will be realised by most of humanity: crosses such as St Mary Castlegate represent an attempt to bring that meaning home before the end of time.

If the cross-face with the bosses at St Mary Castlegate is primarily an evocation of the Second Coming as the fulfilment of the Crucifixion, how might this help with a reading of the face with the animals? Bailey points out that that many Irish crosses have 'their Crucifixion on one side of the cross-head and a scene showing Christ in Judgement on the other', and he compares the Irish carvings with three English stones, from Billingham (Cleveland), Thornton Steward (N. Yorks) and one of the other cross-heads from St Mary Castlegate (Bailey 1980), which is discussed below. A Last Judgement/Second Coming image on one face thus may well be balanced by a Crucifixion image on the other. In this case, images of encompassing dogs, alluding to Psalm 21 and the words spoken by Christ on the Cross, would be highly appropriate. If they are lions, and, as Hawkes argues, lions represent the Risen Christ, the cross would then carry imagery associated with the Resurrection on one face and the Second Coming on the other, the whole contained within the Cross as an evocation of the Crucifixion. Either analysis is doctrinally sound and would make for a powerful visual statement of faith. In either case, whether lions or dogs, this cross-head demonstrates complex and learned iconography and a wide range of reference, both biblical and patristic, hinting at a community of sophisticated patrons and craftsmen.

St Mary Castlegate 3: the Context

The possible inherent meanings of the St Mary Castlegate cross-head are intriguing, but not more so than the possible origins of its motifs. If an Irish or western Scottish origin is postulated for the animal motif, how might it have travelled to St Mary Castlegate?

The Hiberno-Norse settlers in Cumbria and Yorkshire from the early tenth century onwards are usually seen as the vector for the motif of the ring-headed cross: Bailey cites as possible *exempla* for the type St Martin's cross at Iona, the south cross at Clonmacnoise (co. Offaly), and a cluster at Ahenny (co. Tipperary), Killamery and Kilkieran (County Kilkenny), all in the hinterland of Waterford (Bailey 1980). However Mayo, Drumcliff, Donaghmore and Galloon are all in the northern and western parts of Ireland, a long way from the Viking or Hiberno-Norse settlements which, with the exception of Limerick, cluster in the south and east. The usual date given for the beginning of Hiberno-Norse incursions into Cumbria is 902, based on an entry from the *Annals of Ulster*, referring to the expulsion of the heathen from Dublin.

Iona and Islay were undoubtedly part of the region that experienced Viking raids and settlement (Woolf, 2007). Settlement on Islay in particular is suggested by a few furnished burials with Scandinavian-type grave-goods (Graham-Campbell and Batey, 2001). However the available archaeological evidence does no more than indicate that people and ideas were circulating in a Hiberno-Norse milieu that included sites with impressive Christian sculpture.

It is impossible to say whether any of these people were interested in crosses, or whether they had any connexion with York: the evidence is not there. Bailey surveys the arguments about the Manx, Irish or Scottish inspiration for the Northumbrian ring-headed crosses, but goes on to argue that '[t]his dispute about origins is…a side-issue: the important point is that the presence in England of a ring connecting the arms of a cross indicates that we are dealing with a monument of the Viking period' (Bailey 1980). But it surely indicates more than that: it shows that, at St Mary Castlegate and elsewhere, we are dealing with people who had looked *closely* at ring-headed crosses, some of which were a considerable distance from the usual Viking areas; and who had thought those crosses important enough both to remember and to reproduce with considerable skill, not only in their essentials but in some of their minor details. The usual definition of the Hiberno-Norse does not include ecclesiastics, but perhaps we should reconsider or, rather, consider that other people as well as the Hiberno-Norse as usually defined may been travelling between Ireland and Northumbria in the tenth century. The leaders of the Hiberno-Norse were progressively assimilated into Christian practices over the course of the tenth century: Woolf concludes his assessment of the career of Amlaib (Olaf) Cuaran thus: 'He began his career as a pagan plunderer and ended it as a penitent on Iona' (Woolf, 2007). Amlaib ruled twice in York between 941 and 952 and was a major power-player in Dublin, ruling there several times before his abdication and death in 981: what was the long back-story of his relationship with Irish and Ionan monastics?

St Mary Castlegate: the Other Carved Stones

There are two other fragmentary cross-heads from St Mary Castlegate. One of these (4) is also ring-headed, and Lang suggests an early tenth century date, on grounds both of form and of motif. The other (2) is a free-armed cross of a type familiar from the pre-Viking Age. On one face is the crucified Christ with creatures - in one case a serpent - carved beneath His outstretched arms. The other face carries a battered human figure. Lang cites several Northumbrian parallels for the position of Christ (Ellerburn 8, Sinnington 11, Kirkdale 1 and Great Ayton) and suggests that, 'Its origins may well be Irish; in the light of the York-Dublin axis in the tenth century this would not be surprising'.

Coatsworth, too, draws attention to the Irish affiliations of this free-armed cross-head, but she also points out the conservative, Anglian nature of the form (Coatsworth in Wenham *et al.* 1987). She concludes by describing York's sculptors as having 'eclectic and innovative tendencies'. Eclecticism and innovation are surely signs of a mature, well-informed and confident approach to the making of sculpture.

Finally, at St Mary Castlegate, there are the two recumbent grave slabs. Of these, one is a small fragment whose decoration (still carrying some gesso) suggests the tenth century. The other, which is coped, has an elaborate free-armed cross against a background or ring-knots, which Lang suggests could be late ninth- or tenth-century. He draws a close parallel with Sinnington 15, to the extent of ascribing them to the same hand (Lang, 1991). There are thus two close parallels with Sinnington at St Mary Castlegate, though of very different kinds. The two cross-heads (SMC 2 and Sinnington 11), though similar in concept are very different in execution; the coped slabs on the other hand are virtually identical. All Saints, Sinnington, has an exceptional collection of surviving sculpture, with eighteen pieces which date from the late ninth to tenth centuries and include virtually every form common in the period. There are parts of up to eleven cross-shafts, free-arm and ringed cross-heads, a hogback, and the coped grave-cover already noted. Of this Lang notes that it is 'Late Anglian' in style, whereas other pieces are 'Anglo-Scandinavian'. In addition to the Irish parallels suggested for the figure of the crucified Christ (Sinnington 11 cf. e.g. Castledermot, co. Kildare), Lang also suggests that the figures on the cross-shaft Sinnington 1, shown flanking a staff, are similar to those on the Cross of the Scriptures, Clonmacnoise, co. Offaly, 'which is usually interpreted as the founding of a monastery' (Lang, 1991). Sinnington, on the north side of the Vale of Pickering, is one of a dense cluster of churches with remarkable Anglian and Viking Age sculpture, and lies very close to major ecclesiastical sites such as Stonegrave and Lastingham.

Thus at these two linked sites, Sinnington and St Mary Castlegate, we have a similar culture of multiple monuments drawing widely on Insular and Norse decorative traditions. This culture appears to be established before the end of the ninth century, or at least confidently to refer to its inheritance from the Anglian church, and to make very specific references to the sculptural traditions of Ireland and Iona.

Conclusions

Taken as a group, the stones from St Mary Castlegate refer to an astonishingly wide range of traditions. The hypothesized Irish affiliation of the dog/lion creatures on St Mary Castlegate 3 is extremely thought-provoking, especially given the close links with the assemblage at Sinnington, in connexion with which Lang suggests further Irish parallels. But, on reflection, perhaps this should not astonish. Before the Viking Age, the art of the Northumbrian Church was also eclectic, drawing on Mediterranean and Insular traditions, both Germanic and Celtic. The sculpture from St Mary Castlegate looks much less surprising if placed in the context of a Northumbrian Church that, while rocked to its foundations by the Viking onslaughts of the ninth century, still retained a strong sense of its identity and traditions. It also looks less surprising if we allow for the possibility that the ancient links between York and the Irish churches may have continued into the tenth century, albeit transmuted under a new political dispensation. Admittedly, there is no documentary evidence for this hypothesis, but there is very little documentary evidence for any of the activities of the Northumbrian Church at this period. The stones should be allowed to speak for themselves.

Bibliography

Bailey, R. N. 1980. *Viking-Age Sculpture in Northern England*, Collins (London)

Bailey, R. N. 1996. *England's Earliest Sculptors*, Publications of the Dictionary of Old English, 5 (Toronto)

Clemoes, P. and Hughes, K. (eds.) 1971. *England before the Conquest: studies in primary sources presented to Dorothy Whitelock*, Cambridge University Press (Cambridge)

Collingwood, W. G., 1909. `Anglian and Anglo-Danish sculpture at York', *Yorkshire Archaeological Journal*, XX, 149–213

Collingwood, W. G., 1927. *Northumbrian Crosses of the Pre-Norman Age*, Faber & Gwyer (London)

Coatsworth, E. in L. P. Wenham *et al.* 1997. *St Mary Bishophill Junior and St Mary Castlegate* The Archaeology of York 8.2 (London): 161-3

Harbison, P. 1992. *The High Crosses of Ireland* 3 vols. Habelt (Bonn)

Hawkes, J. 2001. 'An Iconography of Identity? The Cross-head from Mayo Abbey' in C. Hourihane (ed.) *From Ireland Coming: Irish Art from the Early Christian to the Late Gothic Period and Its European Context* Princeton University Press (Princeton): 261-76

Hebgin, S. and F. Corrigan, 1960. *St Augustine on the Psalms* Paulist Press (Mahwah, NJ)

Higgitt, J., 1991. 'The non-runic inscriptions', in J. T. Lang, *Corpus of Anglo-Saxon Stone Sculpture*, III, *York and Eastern Yorkshire* (Oxford): 44–7

Hughes K. 1971. 'Evidence for contacts between the churches of the Irish and English from the Synod of Whitby to the Viking age', in P. Clemoes and K. Hughes (eds.), *England before the Conquest: studies in primary sources presented to Dorothy Whitelock*, Cambridge University Press (Cambridge): 49-67

Lang, J. T., 1991. *Corpus of Anglo-Saxon Stone Sculpture*, III, *York and Eastern Yorkshire* (Oxford)

Menache S. 1997. 'Dogs: God's Worst Enemies?', *Society and Animals: Journal of Human-Animal Studies* 5/1: np. <http://www.psyeta.org/sa/sa5.1/menache.html> [Accessed 21 August 2009].

Raw, B. 1990. *Anglo-Saxon Crucifixion Iconography and the Art of the Monastic Revival* Cambridge University Press (Cambridge)

Tweddle, D. in L. P. Wenham *et al*. 1997. *St Mary Bishophill Junior and St Mary Castlegate* The Archaeology of York 8.2 (London): 155-60

Wenham, L. P. *et al*. 1997. *St Mary Bishophill Junior and St Mary Castlegate* The Archaeology of York 8.2 (London)

Woolf, A. 2007. *From Pictland to Alba: 789-1070.* Edinburgh University Press (Edinburgh)

Commemoration at York: the Significance of Minster 42, 'Costaun's' Grave-Cover

Heather Rawlin-Cushing, Ph.D.
Independent Scholar, Suffolk

In 1969, excavations beneath the south transept of York Minster revealed, under the footings and paving of the Norman church, part of a pre-Conquest cemetery (Phillips, 1995, 75-92). Happily, not only did this cemetery contain a large number of undisturbed burials, some very helpful for illuminating aspects of later Anglo-Saxon funerary practices, but a significant number of these graves were surmounted with stone covers and markers, providing an all too rare opportunity to witness an area of Anglo-Saxon cemetery that remained, as it were, frozen almost in its original state (Phillips, 1995, 84; Lang, 1991, 71-6; Lang, 1995, 433-465). This paper focuses on one stone in particular from this cemetery, Minster 42 (Okasha, 1971, 134-5; Lang, 1991, 75-6; Eaton, 2000, 76-7; Figure 1).

Minster 42 stands out from the other stones recovered from the cemetery because it carries inscriptions, one of which is an Anglo-Saxon epitaph, the other a Roman commemorative message, signalling a previous function of the stone. The fact of this monument being a reused Roman stone is not surprising in the context of this cemetery, which lay close to the ruins of the Roman *principia* building, and indeed, many, if not all, of its stones appear to have been crafted from Roman masonry, which must have been in abundance at the site (Hope-Taylor, 1971, 27, 35-9; Norton, 1988, 8; Hall, 2004, 493. On the reuse of Roman masonry during the Anglo-Saxon period, see Stocker & Everson, 1990; Eaton, 2000). What is remarkable, however, is its use of text, both the preservation of the Roman text and the addition of the Anglo-Saxon one; it is the only inscribed gravestone to be recovered from this context at the Minster and, furthermore, is one of only a handful of inscribed stones to survive from Viking-age Northumbria. Despite the dearth of Viking-age inscribed monuments, sculpture production during this period appears, from the extant evidence, to have increased fivefold from the pre-Viking period, and a considerable number of these stones can be identified as having performed a commemorative function on the basis of their form, either as grave covers or markers, or the fact that they were discovered *in situ* above graves, which is why, of course, the discovery of the pre-Conquest Minster cemetery is so important. In a period when the majority of funerary monuments were uninscribed, the choice of an inscription rather than ornamental decoration on a grave cover is certainly worth taking note of.

However, Minster 42 is not a stone without problems. Despite its archaeological context, it is incredibly difficult to date precisely because it has no ornament on which art historical comparisons can be made. On the basis of some of the letterforms used in the inscription and the fact of its discovery above a grave in the latest phases of burial at the Anglo-Saxon Minster, Lang assigned it a broad date range of tenth to eleventh century (Lang, 1991, 75-6). Yet, dating is a key issue when it comes to interpretation of this stone, because it makes a difference to any interpretation of the monument if it was made, for instance, during the first half of the tenth century, when Scandinavian rulers were dominant in York, or whether it was made after 954 and the death of the last Viking ruler, Erik Bloodaxe, when York, officially at least, fell back under English control (see Rollason, 1998, 63-9). This paper addresses some of the questions that Minster 42 poses with regard to its date, the person it commemorated, the choice of text over ornament and in general the practice of commemoration with stone monuments in Viking-age York.

The Inscriptions

The Roman commemorative inscription is arranged in a bordered panel along the length of the slab and has been reconstructed to read (Okasha, 1971, 134-5):

> D(IS) M(ANIBUS) [A]NT(ONI) GARGILIAN[I] EQU(O) | PUBL(ICO) E[X PR]A[E]F(ECTO) LEG(IONIS) (SEXTAE) V(IXIT) AN(NOS) (QUINQUAGINTA SEX) | M(ENSES) (SEX) CLA(UDIUS) FLORENTINUS | DEC(URIO) GENEREIUS

> To the Spirits of the Departed (and) of Antonius Gargilianus, of equestrian status, formerly prefect of the sixth legion. He lived fully fifty-six years, six months. Claudius Florentinus, decurion, his son-in-law (had this made).

This is a common epigraphic formula of the first century onwards, outlining the identity of the deceased and his age at death, as well as the identity of his commemorator, who was probably also his heir (see Adams and Tobler, 2007). The slab was cut from a Roman sarcophagus. This can be verified by comparison with sarcophagi still surviving in the city, some of which carried inscriptions and decoration very similar to that displayed on Minster 42 (see the entries for York in Adams and Tobler's appendices, 2007, 103-217). The slab was cut from the original monolithic monument in such a way that the lower and right edges were truncated, while the left retained its full length. This accounts for the off-centre appearance of the Roman inscription, which would originally have been centred on the side of the sarcophagus. The plain section to the left has been appropriated for the later inscription, which reads at right angles to the former and indicates that this was the head of the slab in its secondary position.

The Anglo-Saxon inscription is preceded by a cross and follows a formula that relates to pre-Viking monastic epitaph forms, beginning *Orate pro anima*, 'Pray for the soul of...':

+ORATEP
OANIMA
COSTAVN
C

This epitaph formula is found in fragmentary form on another monument from the Minster (Minster 21) (Okasha, 1971, 133; Lang, 1991, 65-6), as well as on a fragmentary cross slab from Billingham, County Durham (Billingham 13; Okasha, 1971, 52-3; Cramp, 1984, 51-2), two 'name stones' from Hartlepool, County Durham (Hartlepool 4 and 5; Okasha, 1971, 77-8; Cramp, 1984, 99-100), and two shaft fragments from Lancaster (Collingwood, 1927, 59; Okasha, 1971, 89-90). The Lancaster shafts date to the first half of the ninth century and the other pieces date broadly to the eighth, meaning that they cannot be used as direct comparatives with Minster 42, which corresponds to a Viking-age phase of burial at York. That is not to conclude, however, that these early stones could not have provided a form of epigraphic model for Minster 42 and it is possible that the choice of wording on this monument was just as important as the use of text to communicate a commemorative message and the choice of the previously inscribed stone itself.

On Minster 42 the name of the commemorated individual appears to be 'Costaun', but it may not be complete as the inscription continues into a final line, which is now illegible except for a probable C at the beginning. This name form is not recorded elsewhere, but it has been suggested that it may be English, deriving from the elements Cos- or Gos-, or even a British or Welsh derivation of the name Constans or Constantius (Okasha, 1971, 134). On this basis, it would perhaps not be beyond the realms of probability to suggest that the name could have been a derivation of Constantine. Certainly, however, it does not seem to indicate Scandinavian origins and this fact is perhaps significant in the context of a monument used in Viking-age York.

The amount of wear to the Anglo-Saxon inscription would seem to suggest that it had been exposed to the elements for quite a while before being covered over and preserved by the Norman building work and this stands in favour of a date in the tenth century perhaps more so than the eleventh. It is also fair to argue by the same logic that the Roman inscription, at the time when the stone was adapted for reuse, was considerably more legible than it is now, meaning that it could probably have been read and understood by tenth or eleventh century viewers. This supposes, of course, that the Roman text was left visible at the time of the stone's reuse; certainly no attempts appear to have been made to efface it from the slab, although it is possible that a thick layer of gesso and paint could have effectively hidden it.

This line of argument returns to the question of why this particular stone was chosen rather than a plain building block. Knowing that the slab was cut from a Roman sarcophagus, three key observations can be made that are helpful for understanding the motivations of its later users. Firstly, Roman cemeteries, and consequently Roman funerary monuments, were prohibited by law within the city walls meaning that, as Tim Eaton has pointed out, it is extremely probable that this slab was found and cut from a monument outside the Anglo-Saxon city and transported to the Minster cemetery (Eaton, 2000, 77). This implies that it was not found among the ruins of the *principia* building and used for convenience, but rather was actively sought for the purpose. Secondly, if the Roman inscription had not been required for the Anglo-Saxon monument, the other long side of the sarcophagus could have been cut, or a plainer sarcophagus chosen. Thirdly, excepting its typically classical abbreviations, it is not unreasonable to suggest that this inscription was understandable in essence to those who composed and were able to read the Latin of the later text because of the shared language and because of the context from which it came. It is probable that it was considered particularly appropriate for a grave cover because of this. It should be concluded, therefore, that the inclusion of the Roman text was an integral part of the conception of the Anglo-Saxon monument.

What, therefore, is the significance of this juxtaposing of texts? Did the Roman stone and its inscription hold an intrinsic meaning that the patron of 'Costaun's' monument wanted to exploit? The Anglo-Saxon text is explicitly religious, with its preceding cross and request for prayers, and makes reference to the epitaph forms used in the pre-Viking monasteries of Northumbria, including York. Yet, the choice of text in what might be termed the 'post-monastic' and 'non-literate' period of the Viking-age, says as much about exclusion of viewers as it does about communication of a message. In the first instance, the use of text on a commemorative monument acted to exclude any illiterate viewers from an independent understanding of the commemorative message, although the very existence of text held implications for the social standing of the individual commemorated. In other words, even if a viewer could not read a text, they surely still knew that they were looking at a text and would have been aware of the circumstances that prohibited them from understanding it. On another level, the choice of language meant that viewers who were literate in the vernacular only would be excluded from reading a Latin text, which might be intended to indicate to them that the individual commemorated was monastically educated, or at least had connections close enough with the church to warrant the use of an explicitly religious language for his epitaph.

Viewers of Minster 42 had to be capable of reading both of the Latin inscriptions and understanding that one was contemporary, the other ancient, in order to independently gain a full understanding of the monument. David Stocker has argued, in the case of St Mary le Wigford 6, Lincoln, an inscribed Roman tombstone that has been very conspicuously re-used as an eleventh-century dedication stone, that the juxtaposing of the two texts was a deliberate and explicit manipulation of the past to suit the concerns of the Anglo-Saxon present (Stocker and Everson, 1990, 94; Stocker and Everson, 1999, 214-16). His interpretation of this usage is twofold: on one hand, he infers that "the kudos of the Roman world is being appropriated for church use"; on the other, "that the placing of such a carefully arranged English Christian inscription over the pagan Latin one is a deliberate attempt to show the domination of the latter by the former" (Stocker and Everson, 1990, 94). A date in the early to mid eleventh century makes St Mary-le-Wigford 6 broadly contemporary with Minster 42 and may indicate a pre-Conquest vogue for the re-use of Roman inscribed stones.

The similarities between the two pieces are clear, although certain differences between them are also significant. First and foremost, it is important to note that the context of re-use at Lincoln is decidedly different from that at York; while Minster 42 was adapted for use as a grave cover, an object with a very intimate connection to one particular person, namely Costaun, the St Mary-le-Wigford stone was employed as the dedication stone of the church and displayed in the church wall beside the door, ensuring that all who passed into the church had the opportunity to see it. Secondly, whereas the secondary York text was composed in Latin, thereby forming a link with the older inscription, the Anglo-Saxon text of the Lincoln monument was written in Old English, making explicit its difference from the older message.

Stocker is surely right to believe that the later text at St Mary-le-Wigford was intended as a usurpation and Christianisation of the earlier one, but this interpretation does not necessarily fit with the context of Minster 42. The fact that a Roman funerary monument was specifically adapted to fit a secondary funerary context and that the choice of a Latin text complements the Latin of the earlier inscription, suggests more that similarities were intended to be seen between the past and the present in the context of 'Costaun's' life and death. The placement of the Anglo-Saxon inscription at right angles to the Latin seems to be borne more of convenience in terms of indicating the head of the grave, rather than a desire to establish dominance over the earlier text. It is possible that assumptions were made about the Roman text on the basis that it was written in Latin, to the effect that this particular use of language must have indicated the same religious bias that it demonstrated in the Anglo-Saxon world. Did the patron of Minster 42 assume that the stone he was reusing was the funerary monument of an ancient Christian simply because the epitaph was written in Latin? Alternatively, if the name 'Costaun' was, in fact, a derivative of Constantius or Constantine, the significance of drawing parallels between the Roman and Anglo-Saxon periods at York may have dominated the intentions of the commemorator. The Roman Emperor Constantius I died at York in 306, and his son, Constantine, was appointed in his place, apparently at the same site (*AV*, 2.4), paving the way for the Christianisation of the Empire.

It is, of course, impossible to know what passed through the mind of this Anglo-Saxon patron, but it is clear that this previously inscribed stone was considered suitable and that its old message did not have to be hidden. If the Roman inscription was understood to be an early Christian epitaph, the juxtaposing of an Anglo-Saxon commemorative text with this would make a powerful statement about continuity in the church at York, and, if we were to see this monument as a product of the tenth century, this could be seen as highly significant in a city that was potentially suffering under an influx of pagan invaders and settlers. It is difficult to know what the atmosphere in York was really like during the tenth century, to what extent the population was made up of natives and to what extent foreigners (see Hall, 1994, 42-7 and 119-23; Rollason, 2004, 305-14). Certainly, the city was fought over repeatedly in this period and must frequently have been transformed into a bloody and frightening place for English and Scandinavians alike.

The pre-Conquest Minster Cemetery

We can know something of the influence of the Scandinavian settlement on the city from the other stones that were found in the Minster cemetery. The majority of these stones belong to one group, classified as the York Metropolitan School (YMS), and representing the output of a workshop based in the city (Minster 35-39: Lang, 1991, 72-4). Lang analysed the beast chains and winged bipeds that feature on this group and determined that "the animals epitomise the mixed traditions of York styles of c.900", and that, on the basis of their Scandinavian elements the YMS stones must date to the period of Scandinavian influence in the city, that is from 867 to 954 (Lang, 1991, 39). The animals display details that are strongly associated with Scandinavian ornament, in particular the Jellinge style (see Binns, 1956; Bailey, 1980, 55-7; Lang, 1991, 33-6). This can be seen in the long ear trail, the nose-folds and the spiral scrolled joints. However, in essence the beast chains can be related back to pre-Viking English and Irish motifs, and the winged beasts, specifically, Lang saw as deriving from the dragon form found at Otley (1991, 39). Notably, he commented that, "the long traditions of zoomorphic patterns in both Scandinavian and Insular art approach enough of a similarity in the late ninth and tenth centuries to make ethnic attributions a dubious act of criticism" (1991, 33). Indeed, it would be highly unwise, on the basis of ear trails, nose folds and scrolled joints alone, to claim that these monuments indicated Scandinavian patronage of stone commemorative sculpture; the evidence simply does not provide that information. Yet, these features are undoubtedly present, demonstrating the effect of Scandinavian presence in the city. This can be explained, however, by the probability that the settlers brought with them portable objects bearing these ornamental forms, such as jewellery, weaponry and textiles, and also that they swiftly set up trading links between their base at York and their Continental homeland (MacGregor, 1978, 37). The carvers of the York Metropolitan School appear to have worked with templates and effectively mass-produced, in terms relevant to the conditions of the time, these commemorative monuments, no two exactly the same, but all similar enough to be sure of being recognised as part of the group.

The fact of 'mass production', or at least evidence of organised workshop processes founded on seemingly commercial ethics, is significant in itself. Stones of the YMS group occur across the city (All Saints Pavement 1, St Denys 1 and 2, Clifford Street 1: Lang, 1991, 79-80, 81-2, 102-3), not just at the Minster, and there is also evidence of an outlier at Gainford, County Durham (Gainford 20: Cramp, 1984, 86), which has been taken as support of the practice of commercial export. But none of this can provide firm information about the ethnicity of the patrons of these stones. The discovery of a group of YMS stones in one particular cemetery could be taken as an indication that they were used by a specific social group, or even a family, but distribution across the city and as far afield as Gainford could be seen to speak against this. It may simply be that the YMS stones witness the development of a workshop of carvers in York during the late ninth or first half of the tenth centuries, producing monuments that became fashionable precisely because they drew on traditional ornamental forms of both English and Scandinavian cultures and, therefore, appealed to both potential markets. To say that the stones were specifically produced for Scandinavians on the basis of the Jellinge influences in the beast motifs would be to make a number of unfounded assumptions, not least that the Scandinavians were actively using stone sculpture on a large scale as a method of monumental commemoration. Such use would also imply that the stones, by virtue of their similarity and large numbers, indicated Scandinavian-ness and were used specifically to advertise the ethnicity of patrons and those commemorated.

Furthermore, although their ornament indicates that they were made in the late ninth or first half of the tenth century, during the period of Scandinavian dominance in the city (see Rollason, 1998, 63-9), these stones were not in their primary positions when they were found in the excavations (Kjølbye-Biddle, 1995, 81). The fact that some of the stones had been broken to act as end stones to others of the group, which remain intact, demonstrates that they had been reused. Even some of the covers were reused in fragmentary condition, as is amply demonstrated by Minster 36 and 37, which were discovered above the burial next to that covered by Minster 42. These burials are clearly of a later date than the stones that surmount them, potentially dating anywhere between the mid-tenth and mid-eleventh centuries. The fact that Minster 42 appears in close association with these reused stones would seem, on the face of things, to indicate a similar date for its use.

However, this stone does not seem to have been one that was taken from above a ninth or early tenth century grave and then placed above a later one; its commemorative inscription, more so than the fact that it is unbroken, speaks against this. Minster 42 is an intensely personal monument, much more so than the YMS stones in their secondary positions, and even, it could be argued, in their primary positions because of their general lack of individuality. Although it is practically impossible to know why the YMS stones were reused in the way they were, it can at least be argued that it was their very sameness that made this possible. The fact that they didn't display any explicitly personal commemorative elements, such as inscriptions or figure carvings that might be interpreted as portrait representations of the deceased, meant that they were easily adaptable to new uses. Even in their secondary positions, these stones do not become personal and individual in the same way as Minster 42; they remain the monuments of other people, cut up and rearranged over new graves, and they still lack the originality, and consequently the underlying message, of 'Costaun's' monument.

A great part of the significance of the YMS group of monuments at the Minster and the inscribed Minster 42, however, lies in the fact of their having been discovered *in situ* over burials, and the archaeological evidence of those burials may also be considered as helpful for the overall interpretation of the stones and, in particular, for evidence of the ethnicity of the individuals using them. The excavated graves are, in general, neatly aligned and show evidence of having been arranged in rows. The majority of graves recorded contained uncoffined burials, which may demonstrate that these graves were relatively poor in comparison with those that may have existed nearer the church (Kjølbye-Biddle, 1995, 85). However, the finds of elaborate chest-coffin locks and hinges, and the predominance of stone grave markers, led to the classification of these burials as high status (Kjølbye-Biddle, 1995). It is possible that the cemetery contained a mixture of wealthy and less affluent graves, or the finds may demonstrate the choice between spending money on items for burial with the deceased and structures for commemoration of the grave above ground. Thus, the display of commemorative features in the churchyard could be more important to some than the protection or 'comfort' of the body in the grave.

Two bodies appear to be buried on biers (Kjølbye-Biddle, 1995, 86). One is a child burial, where the body was apparently buried on the narrow plank or board upon which it was carried to the cemetery. The second is that of an adult male, oriented with the head to the east, laid on a wooden structure that may have been part of a boat or cart. This has been interpreted as an example of Scandinavian burial in England; its presence in an area in which stones with Scandinavian influenced designs are used may indicate Scandinavian patronage of those commemorative monuments. However, the fact that these stones have been reused means that their original patrons cannot be known, unless it is assumed that they were reused by descendents of those initially commemorated by them.

Ultimately, the difficulty of determining the patronage of the YMS group of monuments must be admitted; the patronage of the Minster 42, however, seems not to have been Scandinavian. Nevertheless, the evidence of bier burials in relation to these stones has been taken as an indication of Scandinavian burial in this part of the cemetery. The use of domestic storage chests as coffins in some of the graves may be a sign of impoverishment that complements a similar interpretation of the reuse of the YMS stones, although it has been argued that the reuse of the Roman inscribed monument for 'Costaun's' grave cover was a deliberate and significant feature of this stone's commemorative message. It should be noted, however, that the use of domestic chests can also be seen as a display of wealth and status, insomuch as a truly impoverished family may have been more likely to seek a simple uncoffined burial. The choice of a coffin, whatever form it takes, or of a bier, has its own set of status implications when considered in the context of funerary ritual as an opportunity for public display. Similarly, the manner in which the YMS stones were reused, with some broken down to form end stones, perhaps constitutes a more elaborate monumental display than the stones in their original form may have made if they were used on their own and not as part of composite monuments. Certainly, it seems that consciousness of display was not diminished in the secondary use of these stones, even if they are not highly original works.

Textual Commemoration in Viking-age Northumbria

'Costaun's' monument is far from being a lone beacon of individual expression in the commemorative landscape of Viking-age Northumbria. There are three other inscribed monuments from this period and region that demonstrate that a similar form of personalized commemoration was occurring. The first is Monkwearmouth 3 (County Durham), an unusually shaped marker stone, bearing enigmatic figure carvings (Colgrave and Cramp, 1965, 26; Cramp, 1984, 123). Its inscription is rather sketchily incised onto a band moulding on the main face of the slab and comprises the English male name *TidfirÞ* (Page, 1973, 143). Beneath, two figures appear to hold up a box-like object between them. Beneath this object and between the feet of the figures is a small relief cross. There are no facial features or details of dress, although each figure appears to wear a knee-length garment, that on the right, seemingly a skirt. On the reverse of the slab there is a representation of a single figure, apparently depicted in motion, striding to the right. Again there are no facial features and a general lack of attention to any details of dress; this figure could be naked. Hodges' assertion that he carries an object in each hand is probably correct (Hodges, 1906, 16, but see also Cramp, 1984, 123).

This is a mysterious monument. In size and shape, it indicates it probable function as a grave marker, and the incised personal name strengthens this interpretation. Yet, its figure imagery, although given a Christian flavour by the image of the cross, is virtually indecipherable. Cramp's dating for this stone is the first half of the tenth century. Unfortunately, the sources do not reveal whether Monkwearmouth suffered directly at the hands of Viking raiders in the later eighth and ninth centuries (Rollason, 2003, 211-13). Excavation has revealed that the site to the south of the present church continued in use throughout the later Anglo-Saxon period as a lay cemetery (Colgrave and Cramp, 1965, 12-13, 26). It is perhaps significant in this context that Monkwearmouth 3 was discovered in this area (Hodges, 1906, 16). This stone can, therefore, be related to a cemetery that was active during the Viking period on the site of a monastery that may not have been fully functional at the time.

The second inscribed monument is Chester-le-Street 1 (County Durham), a freestanding cross shaft, which seems to be the earliest surviving monument from this site, having been dated art historically to the late ninth century; other stones from the site date to the tenth or eleventh centuries (Cramp, 1984, 53-9; but see also Cambridge, 1989, 374, 378-9). The main face displays a figure scene of a man on horseback, wearing a cap-like helmet and carrying a shield. Above, a two-headed beast seems to reach down and threaten the rider. The name Eadmund is inscribed onto the neck of the beast in two uneven lines and in a mixture of runes and Anglo-Saxon letters (Okasha, 1971, 62; Page, 1973, 30, 35, 59, 134-5, 143). This is the only inscribed monument from Chester-le-Street, although there is some doubt as to whether the inscription is part of the original decorative scheme or a later addition (Cramp, 1984, 54). In any case, however, the name seems to be deliberately juxtaposed with the figure of the rider, and suggests to the viewer that this is in fact intended as a 'portrait' representation of the commemorated individual. Beneath this scene are two ring knots. The other three sides of the cross are covered with interlace designs; there are no other animal motifs or human figures.

It is worth noting that the necks of the two beast heads that threaten the rider are smooth and blank apart from the last three letters of the inscription, with no evidence of cutting back or remodelling. These seem to merge into, not a body of the beast as such, but rather a rectangular panel on which the first four letters of the name are positioned, again with no apparent cutting back or remodelling. It seems, therefore, that an inscription in this position, either incised or painted, should be seen as part of the original conception of this monument, although whether the present inscription is contemporary with the shaft's design and production is still potentially debateable. The stone is broken off just above the inscription and there is no indication how large this rectangular panel was formerly; what survives could be the last word of a longer inscription.

It is impossible to state without doubt that the horseman depicted on this shaft is a 'portrait' representation of the man named above, and the inclusion of the beast heads above him certainly transforms this image into the realm of the symbolic, as opposed to a representation from nature. The beast heads are integral to the image of the horse and rider; this is demonstrated by the rather unnerving feature of the beast licking at the ear of the horse. This action seems to constitute a clear threat to both horse and rider. Thompson has recently discussed the notion of dragons and *wyrms* threatening both the living and the dead in Viking Age literature and sculptural imagery (Thompson, 2004, 92-169). In light of her discussion, it is possible to consider that on Chester-le-Street 1 the two-headed beast may be taken as a representation of 'death'; that is, the dead man is depicted as in life but overshadowed by his death in the symbolic form of the beast above.

This interpretation is, of course, speculative, but the depiction of a horseman in conjunction with an inscribed name remains, nevertheless, a tempting prospect for association with a commemorative function. The horseman is surely representative of someone, and if it is accepted that this person is the individual named in the inscription above, the image provides some limited information about the man, or at least about they way he, or his loved ones, wished him to be remembered. Clearly, this man is a warrior; the shield he carries on his left arm demonstrates this. The fact that he is mounted indicates that he is of high rank and status, being able to provide his own warhorse; he is a member of the warrior elite (see Davis, 1989; Harrison, 1993, 12; Underwood, 1999, 146).

This shaft has been classed as transitional, displaying "a combination of Anglian traditions and newer Scandinavian motifs" (Cramp, 1984, 54; also Cambridge, 1989, 374). It appears in a region of Northumbria that was little affected by the mainstream of Scandinavian settlement, although the region, and the church, was subject to some Viking activity in the early tenth century and conflicts over land-holdings. Specifically, this is the new home of the wandering Lindisfarne community, who fled their island monastery to protect themselves and the relics of St Cuthbert from destruction in the Viking attack of 875 (see especially Cambridge, 1989; also Rollason, 1987; Bonner 1989). The stone displays an English personal name in what appears to be a commemorative context and the use of commemorative texts has been shown to be associated particularly with the expression of learning, piety and hereditary status among the Anglo-Saxon elite classes. In these essentials this monument demonstrates elements characteristic of native patronage, production and use. Yet, the motif of an armed warrior on horseback is one more commonly encountered with sculpture produced in areas of Scandinavian settlement.

Forms deriving from the monastic traditions of the northeast should be expected on a piece of sculpture coming from a site associated with the community of St Cuthbert. However, the community also had significant contact with the Scandinavians prior to their settlement at Chester-le-Street, when they were housed at Crayke, near York (Cambridge, 1989, 380f; Rollason, 1987, 51). Following the death of Halfdan in 877 (or 882, according to a later source), Cuthbert's community were instrumental in placing a Christian, or more accurately, recently christianised, Scandinavian ruler in charge of York, in the figure of Guthfrith (*HSC* 13. Also *HED* II.13). It can be argued that the monastic community were attempting to forge a peaceful agreement with the new ruling classes, or that they were trying, and in this case succeeding, in reasserting some of the power that the monastic houses had held over the ruling classes before the invasions. This would also provide a way for native Anglo-Saxons to assert themselves politically, under the guise of a religious cause, in the new political climate. The supposedly Scandinavian elements in the design of Chester-le-Street 1 could derive from this period in the community's history, but this still does not explain why a monument naming an Englishman should also carry an image of an armed rider in the Scandinavian style.

Bonner has discussed the importance of patronage for the community of Chester-le-Street, while Cambridge has convincingly argued that the evidence of the site suggests that the community did not intend to stay there for as long as they did and even suggests that they may have sent their own dead back to Lindisfarne for commemoration (Bonner, 1989; Cambridge, 1989, 372, 379). The shrine of St Cuthbert was a great attraction for wealthy patrons, including the kings of Wessex, most notably Aethelstan, in his campaigns against the Scandinavians in the North (*HSC* 25-7). Rollason has pointed out that the apparent wanderings of the Lindisfarne community with their saint may have been more of an exercise in public relations during a troublesome time than an enforced exile (Rollason, 1987, 58). In this climate, it is not unreasonable to consider that wealthy patrons of the saint may seek burial close to his remains, and would also take the opportunity to advertise the fact through monumental commemoration.

It is possible to consider that the imagery of the mounted warrior was not in itself explicitly Scandinavian, but that it may reflect the concerns of a late-ninth-century native population in the process of assimilating an invading and settling people. That is to say, the imagery can be viewed as a choice for self-representation – explicitly, an armed man on a horse - rather than a display of stylistic influences – implicitly, displaying knowledge or acceptance of foreign motifs. In the second decade of the tenth century, following the Battle of Corbridge (918), land around Chester-le-Street was seized by Ragnald of York and given to one of his followers, Onlafball (*HSC* 22-3). Onlafball did not manage to take the church's lands at Chester-le-Street; he was struck down in his attempt, "and St Cuthbert, as was his right, received his land" (*HSC* 23). Despite the evidence for the Scandinavian occupation of land in the Chester-le-Street area during the tenth century, there is no reason to conclude that the stones from the church were the result of Viking patronage or, for that matter, that they display any motifs that would significantly demonstrate any form of foreign influence in their design. Rather, they show connections with sites well within the sphere of English control centred on Bamburgh. The account of Onlafball's failed attempt to defy the church is an example of the community's hostility towards the newcomer, and should be taken as an indication of tensions between the native population and the settlers. Hadley argues that similar tensions are implied by the Community's well-documented connections with the kings of Wessex (Hadley, 2000, 114-15). It is perhaps not simply the fact that Onlafball was pagan that proved problematic, but more importantly the fact that he was laying claim to church lands, and consequently church revenues. The community of Cuthbert may have become involved in the early appointments of rulers at York, but this episode may have been purely the result of self-interest; it seems to have been integral to their securing lands at Chester-le-Street. Once settled, whether they intended to stay long or not, they attracted considerable levels of English patronage, and surely remained quintessentially English, their church at Chester-le-Street acting as a bastion of the old monastic tradition.

The third inscribed monument is different again. It is Gainford 21 (County Durham), a fragment of what appears to have been an otherwise plain upright grave marker, with an inscription running along at least one of its narrow sides, reading *Alrihc settae...* in Anglo-Saxon letters (Okasha, 1971, 73; Cramp, 1984, 87). The name Alrihc is probably English and the inscription seems to follow a typically pre-Viking epitaph formula that runs along the lines of *X settae Þis becun aefter Y*, 'X set up this monument in memory of Y', found on ninth-century monuments from Thornhill (West Yorkshire), Yarm and Wycliffe (North Yorkshire), Urswick (Lancashire) and Falston (Northumberland). On these pieces, the formula seems to indicate lay patronage and concerns about social standing and heredity (Rawlin-Cushing, 2009; 2010). The *Corpus* dating for Gainford 21 is broad, between the mid-ninth and mid-eleventh centuries, as there is no ornamental detail on the stone by which it could be dated art historically. There is no evidence that sculpture was being produced at this site in the pre-Viking period.

Gainford was originally a royal vill, gifted to the community of St Cuthbert in 830 by Ecgred, bishop of Lindisfarne (830-845), meaning that the church on this site was still relatively young when the Vikings started settling in the late 860s and 870s. Symeon of Durham relates that in the early tenth century the estate formed part of the lands seized by Ragnald after the second Battle of Corbridge and given to another of his followers in a mirroring of the Onlafball episode (*HED* II.5). It should also be noted that Gainford, nestling on the north banks of the River Tees, sits just on the outskirts of the main region of Scandinavian settlement north of York.

The slab could be one of the first pieces of stone sculpture to be made at the site; its use of text may herald a connection with the monastic traditions of Lindisfarne community, who held the estate from c.830. The formula is not encountered on any monuments that can be dated with confidence to the tenth century or later. It makes sense, therefore, that the formula appearing at Gainford should be considered to have been used within, or at least not long after, the period in which it was being used at other sites, rather than to suggest that it appeared as an antiquated reference to earlier elite expressions. A date for this monument in the second half of the ninth century seems preferable to one in the first half of the eleventh, and this consequently indicates that this stone demonstrates the practice of burial and commemoration along traditional lines at this site during the first half century of its establishment.

The message of each of these three monuments should be considered in the context of what is known of Scandinavian activity in and around the sites of their production. At Monkwearmouth, the enigmatic figure scenes display some form of activity that is clearly of a Christian relevance; this at a site that must have been aware of, and possibly directly affected by, Viking activities along the northeast coast in the ninth century. At Chester-le-Street, an English man's name is inscribed above a depiction of a mounted warrior, threatened by a dragon-like beast; this at a site which existed as a direct result of Viking attacks and which, in the early tenth century fended off the threat of attack by the pagan, Onlafball. At Gainford, a commemorative epitaph formula that seems to have deliberately emphasised familial ties and hereditary rights among the Anglo-Saxon nobility in the pre-Viking period is used at a site which lay in the borderlands of Scandinavian control and which Ragnald attempted to sequester for one of his followers in the early tenth century. The apparent relationships between these circumstances and the imagery and texts of the monuments may be no more than coincidence, but they are nevertheless worthy of attention. In circumstances which can be interpreted as, at the very least, trying for the native populations of these sites, but were in reality probably intensely frightening and even life-changing for those directly involved, these stones are testament to individuals who saw relevance, possibly necessity, in the clear and permanent identification of their ethnicity, status, religious beliefs and heritage.

Conclusions

Minster 42 is also clearly a very independent expression of identity and can similarly be related to a period of time that was dominated by ethnic diversity and racial power struggles. Yet, its dating is imprecise. In the first place there is the evidence of the inscription, the form of which relates to earlier inscriptions at the site, and the level of wear on the stone also suggests that it was exposed for quite a while before being covered by the Norman work. The close proximity of this grave to others, which were marked by the YMS stones, suggests that they were laid at roughly the same time, but this doesn't have to be the case. It is notable that when found the YMS stones were sandwiched between Minster 42 and the totally plain Minster 44, a pair that seem to have more affinity than, say, Minster 42 and any of the YMS stones. Were these two monuments already in place before the grave between them was cut? Indeed, we must still question why it was considered desirable or necessary to reuse the YMS stones. Did a lack of space in the cemetery maybe lead to their being lifted in order for the ground occupied by the earlier burials to be reused? Were new graves squeezed in wherever possible and these stones reused for want of anything better to do with them? Could it be that they were reused at a time when a carvers' workshop was not operating in the city and if so what impact might that have on the dating of Minster 42? What level of skill was required for the carving of its inscription: could this have been carved by, for instance, one of the YMS carvers following a text, or did the carver himself have to be literate?

Such a barrage of questions so late in the paper seems worthy of an apology, but illustrates amply that Minster 42 really is the epitome of an artefact that raises more questions than it can possibly answer. Ironically, we have to blame for this the very fact that it was discovered *in situ*; had it not been it probably would have been dated considerably earlier or later and its connection, or lack of connection, with the YMS stones would not be cause for debate. However, there is one aspect of Minster 42 that can be argued with some degree of certainty. Whoever was responsible for the design and erection of this monument wanted to communicate a particular message, and it looks very much as if that message was one of superiority, not necessarily in a negative sense, but certainly in a manner in which it was made clear that 'Costaun', the individual being remembered, was familiar with the Latin language, indicating education and more specifically a religious education, that he was devoutly religious, that he or his commemorators had the wherewithal to have such an individual monument made, and that their message related not only to the present time, but looked back to signs of a Christian past at York, perhaps even stressing links with the first Christian emperor, Constantine, who began his reign in the city. This seems without doubt to indicate, regardless of precise dating, a lone voice among the rather multicultural stones of the Minster cemetery, crying out the heritage of the English church. It is possible that the jumbled messages communicated by the Minster stones should be taken quite simply as a reflection of the multicultural nature of the city of York during the tenth and eleventh centuries, and as a measure of diversifying expressions of social and religious identity in a society that had struggled with both conflict and assimilation.

Acknowledgements

I am grateful to Victoria Thompson, David Stocker and Jane Hawkes for helpful comments and suggestions on various aspects of this research.

Abbreviations

AV Anonymous Valensianus
HED Historia Ecclesiae Dunhelmensia
HSC Historia Sacto Cuthberto

Bibliography

Adams, G. W. & Tobler, R. 2007. *Romano-British Tombstones Between the 1st and 3rd Centuries AD: Epigraphy, Gender and Familial Relations*, BAR Publishing (Oxford)

Bailey, R. N. 1980. *Viking-Age Sculpture in Northern England*, Collins (London)

Binns, A. L. 1956. "Tenth-century carvings from Yorkshire and the Jellinge style", *Universitetet i Bergen Årbok, 1956, historisk-antikvarisk rekke*, 2, Bergen

Bonner, G. 1989. "St Cuthbert at Chester-le-Street", in G. Bonner, D. Rollason & C. Stancliffe (ed), *St Cuthbert, His Cult and His Community to AD 1200*, Boydell (Woodbridge): 387-96

Cambridge, E. 1989. "Why did the community of St Cuthbert settle at Chester-le-Street?", in G. Bonner, D. Rollason & C. Stancliffe (ed), *St Cuthbert, His Cult and His Community to AD 1200*, Boydell (Woodbridge): 367-86

Colgrave, B. & Cramp, R. 1965. *St Peter's Church, Wearmouth*, British Publishing Co. (Gloucester)

Collingwood, W. G. 1927. *Northumbrian Crosses of the pre-Norman Age*, Faber & Gwyer (London)

Cramp, R. 1984. *Corpus of Anglo-Saxon Stone Sculpture I: County Durham and Northumberland*, Oxford University Press (Oxford)

Davis, R. H. C. 1989. "Did the Anglo-Saxons have warhorses?", in S. C. Hawkes (ed), *Weapons and Warfare in Anglo-Saxon England*, Oxford University Committee for Archaeology (Oxford): 141-4

Eaton, T. 2000. *Plundering the Past: Roman Stonework in Medieval Britain*, Tempus (Stroud)

Hadley, D. M. 2000. "'Hamlet and the Princes of Denmark': Lordship in the Danelaw, c.860-954", in D. M. Hadley & J. D. Richards (ed), *Cultures in Contact: Scandinavian Settlement in England in the Ninth and Tenth Centuries*, Brepols (Turnhout)

Hall, R. A. 1994. *English Heritage Book of Viking-Age York*, English Heritage (London)

Hall, R. A. 2004. "The topography of Anglo-Scandinavian York", in R. A. Hall (ed), *Aspects of Anglo-Scandinavian York*, Council for British Archaeology (York): 488-97

Harrison, M. 1993. *Anglo-Saxon Thegn AD 449-1066*, Osprey History (Oxford)

Hodges, C. C. 1906. "The memorial stone, supposed to be that of Tidfirth, the last bishop of Hexham", *Antiquaries of Sunderland* 7: 13-16

Hope-Taylor, B. 1971. *Under York Minster: Archaeological Discoveries 1966-1971*, Dean and Chapter of York (York)

Kjølbye-Biddle, B. 1995. "Iron-bound coffins and coffin fittings from the pre-Norman cemetery", in A. D. Phillips and B. Heywood (ed), *Excavations at York Minster, Vol I: From Roman Fortress to Norman Cathedral*, Royal Commission on the Historical Monuments of England (London): 489-521

Lang, J. 1991. *Corpus of Anglo-Saxon Stone Sculpture III: York and Eastern Yorkshire*, Oxford University Press (Oxford)

Lang, J. 1995. "Pre- Conquest sculpture", in A. D. Phillips and B. Heywood (ed), *Excavations at York Minster, Vol I: From Roman Fortress to Norman Cathedral*, Royal Commission on the Historical Monuments of England (London): 433-467

MacGregor, A. 1978. "Industry and commerce in Anglo-Scandinavian York", in R. A. Hall (ed), *Viking Age York and the North*, CBA Research Report 27: 37-57

Norton, C. 1988. "The Anglo-Saxon cathedral at York and the topography of the Anglian city", *Journal of the British Archaeological Association*, 151: 1-42

Okasha, E. 1971. *Hand-List of Anglo-Saxon Non-Runic Inscriptions*, Cambridge University Press (Cambridge)

Page, R. I. 1973. *An Introduction to English Runes*, Methuen & Co (London)

Phillips, A. D. 1995. "The excavations", in A. D. Phillips and B. Heywood (ed), *Excavations at York Minster, Vol I: From Roman Fortress to Norman Cathedral*, Royal Commission on the Historical Monuments of England (London): 33-176

Rawlin-Cushing, H. 2009; 2010. "Sacred and profane: contextualising mixed messages on the Urswick cross: Norse mythology and Christian Iconography", in L. Sever (ed.), *Exploring Lancashire's Sacred Sites: From Prehistory to the Viking Age*, Tempus (Stroud)

Rollason, D. W. 1987. "The wanderings of St Cuthbert", in D. W. Rollason (ed), *Cuthbert, Saint and Patron*, Dean and Chapter of Durham (Durham)

Rollason, D. W. 1998. *Sources for York History to AD 1100*, The Archaeology of York I (York)

Rollason, D. W. 2003. *Northumbria, 500-1100. Creation and Destruction of a Kingdom*, Cambridge University Press (Cambridge)

Rollason, D. W. 2004. "Anglo-Scandinavian York: the evidence of historical sources", in R. A. Hall (ed), *Aspects of Anglo-Scandinavian York*, Council for British Archaeology (York): 305-24

Stocker, D. & Everson, P. 1990. "Rubbish recycled: a study of the re-use of stone in Lincolnshire", in D. Parsons (ed), *Stone. Quarrying and Building in England AD 43-1525*, Phillimore (Chichester)

Stocker, D. & Everson, P. 1999. *Corpus of Anglo-Saxon Stone Sculpture V: Lincolnshire*, Oxford University Press (Oxford)

Thompson, V. 2004. *Dying and Death in Late Anglo-Saxon England*, Boydell (Woodbridge)

Underwood, R. 1999. *Anglo-Saxon Weapons and Warfare*, Tempus (Stroud)

Aspects of the Anglo-Saxon Tradition in Architectural Sculpture and Articulation: the 'Overlap' and Beyond

Prof. Malcolm Thurlby
York University, Toronto

Introduction

The concept of the continuity of aspects of Anglo-Saxon architectural sculpture and articulation after the Conquest is nothing new. In many cases, however, investigation of architectural sculpture has been undertaken without due consideration of its setting. Here it is proposed to examine the sculpture in its architectural context so as to provide a basis for dating other than sculptural style, iconography and technique. This approach applies Eric Fernie's (1977, 385) principle of architectural synthesis, as opposed to architectural analysis, in which it is assumed that a building is of a single date unless there is unequivocal evidence to the contrary. In the absence of documentation, the work will be dated with reference to the latest feature in the original building. The churches of Bibury (Gloucestershire), Langford (Oxfordshire), Milborne Port (Somerset), Knook (Wiltshire), Egleton (Rutland) and Kirkburn (Yorkshire) are investigated in detail, while some later 12th and early 13th-century examples are briefly considered.

Bibury

The early fabric of St Mary at Bibury, including the carved capitals of the chancel arch, is traditionally dated before the Conquest (Keyser 1918-19, 180; Brown 1925, 444; Bird 1928, 45-46; Clapham 1930, 109n, 130, 135, 139; Croome 1953, 7; Taylor & Taylor 1965, 63-66; Taylor and Taylor 1966, 8-9; Heighway 1987, 113; Verey and Brooks 2002, 167-168). Clapham (1930, 130) drew attention to Carolingian-inspired acanthus foliage of so-called Winchester School manuscripts on one of the Bibury capitals. The Taylors (1966, 8-9) called the capitals Ringerike in style and dated them to the early 11th century. George Zarnecki (1955, 1-2) opted for a mid-11th-century date and, like Clapham, associated the two-dimensional foliage with the Winchester acanthus in illuminated manuscripts. Specifically, he compared the south capital with the Arenberg Gospels fol. 108 verso (New York, Pierpont Morgan Library M. 869). He once again commented (1966, 191) on the two-dimensional nature of the carving the effect of which could have been equally well achieved with painting. Later (1978a, 41) he compared the foliage of the south capital at Bibury with capital S2 of the arch to the east chapel of the south transept at Worcester Cathedral, 1084-1089. The form of the Bibury capitals (fig. 1), however, is quite different from the foliated cushions at Worcester.

Their trapezoidal shape, if not the exact form of the foliage, is paralleled in pre-Conquest manuscripts, such as Oxford, Bodleian Library MS Junius II, p. 57 (Temple 1976, cat. 58, fig. 192), and Warsaw, Biblioteka Narowoda MS I. 3311, fol. 15 (Temple 1976, cat. 92, ill. 283). The ribbon-like foliage and horizontal line through the Bibury north capital (fig. 1) may be compared with the border of folio 104 verso of Oxford, Wadham College, MS A.10.22, datable to the late 11th century (Kauffmann 1975, cat. 5, ill. 18). Architecturally, the shape of the Bibury capitals is related to those in the external blind arcade on the nave and chancel of St Laurence at Bradford-on-Avon (Wiltshire) and the upper range of pilasters on the south wall of the chancel at Milborne Port (Somerset) (fig 5). The former may be associated with King Ethelred's gift of the manor and monasterium of Bradford-on-Avon to Shaftesbury abbey (Fernie 1983, 149), while Milborne Port is probably late 11th century (see below; Zarnecki 1966, 98-99; Blair 1985, 134; Gem 1988, 27). The Bibury capitals are set atop the plain jambs of the chancel arch. This follows a pre-Conquest tradition as in the west doorway of the west tower of All Saints at Earls Barton (Northamptonshire) (Fernie 1983, ill 87), and is quite different from the usual arrangement in Normandy where carved capitals are set atop shafts (Bayle 1991). It is also significant that the capitals and abaci at Bibury are carved on through stones in a pre-Conquest tradition. The abacus of the north capital has a quirked hollow chamfer (fig. 1). On the one hand, this may be seen in relation to the pre-Conquest imposts of the former south doorway of St Mary the Virgin at Limpley Stoke (Wiltshire) on which there are two quirks to either side of a narrow roll and above a chamfer (Cramp 2006, 200-221, ills 464-467). On the other hand, the chamfer at Limpley Stoke is not hollow and, more importantly, it is on an impost as opposed to a moulded abacus above a carved capital, as at Bibury. This abacus profile is used in Normandy in the second quarter of the 11th century in the abbey church at Bernay (Baylé 1991, 58-70, ills 130-135, 137-140, 173-176 and 180), and in the mid 1060s at Saint-Etienne at Caen (Baylé 1991), and appears in England after the Conquest in the crypt of Winchester Cathedral, commenced in 1079 (Clapham 1934, 121). At Worcester Cathedral quirked chamfered abaci are used extensively in the crypt but hollow chamfers are confined to the abaci of the slype

Fig. 1. Bibury (Gloucestershire), St Mary, chancel arch, north capital (© M. Thurlby, 2009).

blind arcades where the quirk is omitted. Quite what this means for the date of the Bibury capitals is not easily determined. There is nothing in the earliest fabric at Bibury which can be associated unequivocally with a date after the Conquest. While the present fabric of Worcester Cathedral was commenced in 1084, Philip Barker (1994, 32, 40) suggested that many of the capitals, shafts and bases of the crypt and slype were reused from the Anglo-Saxon church. Be that as it may, given the more precise parallel of the Bibury north abacus with the Winchester profile, a date in the 1080s for Bibury seems most plausible. Domesday records that Bibury belonged to Wulfstan, Bishop of Worcester (1062-1095) (Moore 1982, 3.4). According to William of Malmesbury, Wulfstan built or rebuilt many churches throughout his diocese (Darlington 1928, xxxiv, 21, 52; Gem 1988, 23; Brooks 2005, 15) and Bibury may have been one of them. It may be objected that, with the exception of the quirked hollow-chamfer abacus, Bibury incorporates none of the latest Anglo-Norman motifs and techniques that are used at Worcester Cathedral. However, this very duality of Anglo-Saxon continuity in minor buildings as opposed to Anglo-Norman innovation in the great church is witnessed in the patronage of Bishop William of St Calais (1081-1096) at Norton (Co. Durham) versus Durham Cathedral (Cambridge, 1994, 145-148), and under Bishop Herbert de Losinga (1091-1119) at St Nicholas at Great Yarmouth (Norfolk) versus Norwich Cathedral (Batcock 1988, 188-189, fig. 81).

Langford

Like the Bibury chancel arch capitals, the foliage on and above the belfry capitals of the central axial tower at Langford (Oxon), has been related to pre-Conquest 'Winchester' manuscripts (Clapham 1930, 130; Tweddle 1995, 66, 215). Clapham (1930, 130) also referred to the slender figures supporting the defaced sundial on the south face of the Langford tower, 'which from its architectural detail cannot long have preceded the Norman Conquest'. In addition there is a projecting animal head in the middle of the north face of the tower immediately below the belfry (fig. 2). Inside, the ground floor of the tower is barrel vaulted and there is a clear distinction between the articulation of the east and west arches (fig. 3).

Baldwin Brown (1925, 346, 463) dated the tower to period C3 (1050-1100) and also referred to it as post-Conquest. The Taylors (1965, 367-372) opted for period C3 and also included the capitals and the dancing figures in their catalogue of pre-Conquest sculpture (1966, 20-21, 37). Zarnecki (1966, 91) considered that Langford was 'built about the time of the Conquest', while Gem (1984, 266) opted for a date around 1090. Blair (1994, 175) argued that the patron is Aelfsige of Faringdon, an Englishman who in the time of King Edward owned two hides at Littleworth in Great Faringdon (Berks.). He prospered after the Conquest and amongst extensive new holdings he had 15 hides at Langford by 1086 (Morris

Fig. 2. Langford (Oxfordshire), St Matthew, axial tower, N wall, detail of prokrossos below belfry (© M. Thurlby, 2010).

Fig. 3. Langford, axial tower, interior from SW (© M. Thurlby, 2010).

1978). Tweddle (1995, 215) did not comment on Blair's dating, which may not have been published at the time he was writing, and observed that the 'architectural features of the belfry stage suggest a date for the tower no earlier than the middle of the eleventh century'.

The frieze-like spread of the foliage from the belfry capitals on to the adjacent section of the jambs at Langford is quite different from the Norman tradition in which the sculpture is kept within the confines of the capital. Tweddle's (1995, 66) parallels for the Langford foliage in pre-Conquest manuscripts are entirely convincing but his comparisons with Sompting and Bernay for sculpture continued from the capital on to the narrow imposts are not accurate. At Sompting the motifs that flank the capital are not the same as on the capital (Tweddle 1995, ills 186 and 190), while at Bernay (Baylé 1980, 33, fig 4; Baylé 1991, pls 159-161; Baylé 1992, 76-78, ill. 38) the composition is entirely different. The arrangement at Langford is more closely allied to the capitals of the arch to the west tower at St Bene'ts, Cambridge (Gem 1984, fig. 10), and the arch to the west tower at Barnack (Northamptonshire) (Fernie 1983, fig. 80). In these two instances, the capitals are moulded rather than being carved with foliage but moulded capitals are used on the north belfry openings at Langford (Tweddle 1995, ills 309-312). It is also worth noting that something similar appears in the capitals of the compound piers in the nave of Saint-Vincent at Soignies (Hainault) (Barral I Altet 1989, pls 49 and 50), although the nature of the relationship between Soignies and the English work is not easily determined. Whether or not the Langford north belfry capitals were painted with a foliage pattern like the carving on the belfry openings on the other sides of the tower, or were left plain because the north side of the tower was not in the usual public view, is a moot point. Be that as it may, it is important to record the close relationship between sculpture and painting in the Anglo-Saxon period, as witnessed, for example with the painted angels at Nether Wallop (Hants) (Gem and Tudor-Craig 1981; Tudor-Craig 1990) and the carved angels at St Laurence at Bradford-on-Avon (Cramp 2006). The label stops and hood mould of the chancel arch at Deerhurst (Gloucestershire) still bear distinct traces of paint and there are remains of a painted figure on one of the panels above the chancel arch there (Bagshaw, Bryant and Hare 2006; Gem and Howe 2008). Many examples of foliage above the capitals in Anglo-Saxon manuscripts have been collected by Tweddle (1995, fig. 20) to which we should add the examples in the architectural frame of Rabanus Maurus offering his book to Pope Gregory (Cambridge, Trinity College B. 16. 3, fol. 1 verso; Temple 1976, cat. 14, ill. 48). This juxtaposition is not found in Normandy yet is analogous to the arrangement in the arch from the nave to the west tower at St Bene'ts, Cambridge, where an animal sits on top of each of the abaci. The heavy soffit and frontal rolls in the belfry arches relate most closely to the chancel arch at Wittering (Northamptonshire) and Clayton (Sussex), of which the former is surely built before 1083 when Barnack stone was used for Norman Ely Cathedral.

Zarnecki (1966, 91) observed that the panel with the 'dancing' figures supporting a sundial 'is inserted into the pilaster below the windows in a casual way, unrelated to the string course or the windows'. The setting recalls that of the foliage panels on the west tower at Barnack. Tweddle (1995, 214), compared the figures with the Presentation scene in the Foundation Charter of the New Minster dated 966 (Temple 1976, no. 48, ills 155-6) and the illustrations of the Labours of the Month in BL MS Cotton Tiberius B. V. (Temple 1976, no. 87, ills 273-4). He concluded 'that the sundial came originally from an earlier fabric, and has been reused in its present location'. It is surely more likely that it is contemporary with the tower.

The projecting head on the north wall of the tower (fig. 2) relates to pre-Conquest examples on the west tower at Deerhurst and Barnack. After the Conquest the motif is used above the north transept doorway at Norwich Cathedral, commenced 1096, and on the west wall of the nave at Kilpeck (Herefordshire) *circa* 1134 (Thurlby 1999). The motif is therefore of little help with the date of the Langford tower.

Turning to the interior, the articulation of the west arch of the tower is in a pre-Conquest technique complete with through stones (fig. 3). Through stones are also used for the capitals of the east arch of the tower. Here the form of the capital is paralleled on a grave marker from Winchester Old Minster of the first half of the 11th century (Tweddle 1995, 276-277, ill. 508), and in the Romanesque main arcade capitals of the great Benedictine abbey churches of St Peter at Gloucester and St Mary at Tewkesbury in the last decade of the 11th century. It is worth noting that some large stones are used in the Gloucester choir arcade capitals. The quirked chamfer on the abaci of the Langford capitals first appears in Odda's Chapel at Deerhurst by 1056 (Fernie 1983, 159). The base mouldings of the tower east arch are close to Evesham abbey, commenced in 1077 (Rigold 1977, 113, fig. 3 no. 46). The more elaborate articulation of the east tower arch complete with painted decoration on the shafts, suggests that the arch is at the entry to the sanctuary. The vault beneath the tower probably marks the liturgical choir and is surely contemporary with the building rather than 13th century as suggested by the Taylors (1965, 370); a 13th-century vault would most likely have been ribbed. The Taylors (1965, 370-371) also believed that three-foot gap between the extrados of the vault and the doorways which open to the east and west argued against assigning an Anglo-Saxon date to the vault. However, the same gap is found between the extrados of the presbytery vault and the doorway in the east wall of the crossing tower at Ewenny priory, and here there can be no doubt that these features both belong to the original Romanesque fabric.

While there is nothing in the fabric at Langford that absolutely dates it after 1066, Aelfsige of Faringdon's increased prosperity after the Conquest indicates that a date around 1080 is most likely. This fits happily with the base mouldings of the tower east arch.

Milborne Port

Baldwin Brown (1925, 241, 428, 470) believed that Milborne Port was 'a distinctly Norman building' but that the south wall of the chancel retained 'unmistakable reminiscences of Saxon pilaster strips' (1925, 470). Similarly, Pevsner (1958, 19-20, 237-238) saw Anglo-Saxon and Norman motifs 'indivisibly connected,...a case of the "Saxo-Norman overlap" rather than of Saxon architecture – new motifs used by men familiar with the old' (Pevsner 1958, 20). Against this Taylor and Taylor (1965, 424-428; 1966, 39-40) proposed that the nave south doorway was inserted into earlier fabric, and the stair turret in the angle of the south transept and the south nave wall was a later addition. Zarnecki (1966, 98) disagreed with the Taylors' view that the south nave doorway was inserted; for him 'the building and the doorway are post-Conquest, dating from about 1090 or even a little later. Zarnecki (1966, 99) stated that of the 30 crossing capitals 16 are original and the remainder are 19th-century stucco, while for Foster (1987, 66) the question as to whether the stucco capitals are 11th or 19th century is debatable. Zarnecki convincingly related the foliage on the crossing capitals to that framing the tympanum of the south doorway. In spite of this integrated approach, the account in the *Victoria County History* (Currie 1999, 154) reiterated the Taylors' view that the south doorway was inserted in the 12th century at the same time as the middle stage of the tower was built along with and the staircase which gives access to it. Gem (1988, 27) adopted Zarnecki's dating of the sculpture to the late 11th century and applied this as a whole to the building that welded together pre- and post-Conquest forms 'into an articulate and satisfying whole'. Fernie (2000, 214) also dated the crossing capitals to the late 11th century by style. He listed Anglo-Saxon and Norman elements at Milborne Port and concluded that the church 'is not a misunderstood Anglo-Saxon version of Norman forms, but a combination of the best of both traditions'. Most recently, Cramp (2006, 191-192), stated that '[a]lthough a case can be made for part of the fabric of the church to be pre-Conquest, the rich decoration of its openings appear to be post-Conquest but with strong influence from pre-Conquest art'.

There can be no doubt that Baldwin Brown, Pevsner, Zarnecki, Gem and Fernie are correct is their integrated reading of the late 11th-century fabric of Milborne Port. Further observations serve to substantiate the case. Zarnecki's comparison of the foliage on the tympanum of the south doorway with that of the crossing capitals may be extended to the capitals of the external pilasters on the south wall of the choir and the one remaining foliage capital on the blocked south choir window (figs 4-6).

The latter capital also has a thin plain rim at the top - rather than a fully articulated abacus – like the capitals of the north, south and west crossing arches.

The window arch has a quadrant roll moulding like the north and south crossing arches. Throughout, the tooling of the ashlar belongs to a Norman tradition. The remaining arch of the original external arcade on the north side of the crossing tower also has a quadrant roll moulding and band capitals like those of the crossing piers (fig. 7).

Fig. 4. Milborne Port (Somerset), St John the Evangelist, W crossing arch, N capitals (© M. Thurlby, 2010).

Fig. 5. Milborne Port, S choir exterior capitals (© M. Thurlby, 2009).

Fig. 6. Milborne Port, S choir window interior, detail E capital (© M. Thurlby, 2010).

Fig. 7. Milborne Port, crossing tower, N wall, detail of arcade (© M. Thurlby, 2010).

Fig. 8. Milborne Port, nave and south transept, exterior from SSW (© M. Thurlby, 2010).

Fig. 9. Milborne Port. Milborne Port, crossing, interior to S (© M. Thurlby, 2010).

there can be little doubt that he was responsible for the construction.

This frieze-like arrangement of the capitals is analogous to the belfry capitals at Langford, while the quadrant roll moulding is paralleled in the wall arches of the presbytery aisles at St Peter's abbey, Gloucester, commenced in 1089. The depressed trajectory of the north and south crossing arches may be associated with the upper chapel of St Mary Magdalene in the Bishop's Chapel at Hereford Cathedral erected by Bishop Robert de Losinga, 1079-1095 (Gem 1986). The reticulated masonry on the stair turret in the angle of the south transept and the south wall of the nave (fig. 8) relates to the east wall of the reredorter and west wall of the refectory of Westminster abbey, probably of the 1070s or 1080s (RCHME 1924, pl. 176), and the tympanum of the east doorway to the Great Tower of Chepstow Castle, 1068-1071 (Thurlby 2006, 6, 17, fig. 7).

The vice was originally entered from a doorway in the west wall of the south transept which can still be seen from within the turret. That the stair turret is part of the original scheme is demonstrated by the setting of the south crossing arch which is offset to the east to provide sufficient space for the vice against the south wall of the tower (fig. 9).

Aside from the salient angles of the crossing tower and the triangular blind arches on the former west front of the church which clearly belong to a pre-Conquest tradition, one other aspect of Milborne Port speaks of Anglo-Saxon rather than Norman heritage. The subtle differences in the placement of the crossing capitals and the overt variety in the bases of the crossing piers are in the spirit of the piers at Holy Trinity, Great Paxton (Cambridgeshire) and the different openings in the stair turret of the west tower at All Saints, Hough-on-the-Hill (Lincolnshire) (Taylor & Taylor 1965, 321-324; Stocker & Everson 2006, 6).

In 1086 Milborne Port was held by Reinbald/Regenbald (Thorn & Thorn 1980, 1.10), former chancellor to Edward the Confessor who continued in royal service under William I (Keynes 1987). Blair (1985, 134) and Gem (1988, 27) associate the church with Regenbald and

Knook

The tympanum of the south doorway of St Margaret at Knook (Wiltshire) has been variously dated between 1000 and the early 12th century (fig. 10).

Clapham (1930, 136, fig. 44) dated it to the mid 11th century and compared it with the Aldhelm, De virginitate (London Lambeth Palace Library MS 200 (Part II) of the late 10th or early 11th century (Temple 1976, cat. 39). Subsequently, Clapham (1947, 163), added that the date for the tympanum immediately before the Conquest was 'determined by the character of the capitals of the side shafts of the doorway itself and the capitals of the chancel arch in the building'. Clapham's manuscript comparison was followed by Kendrick (1949, 40-41) who dated the tympanum with the manuscript around 1000. Temple (1976, cat. 39) also referred to Aldhelm manuscript parallel and repeated Kendrick's date of *circa* 1000 for

Fig. 10. Knook (Wiltshire), St Margaret, S doorway (© M. Thurlby, 2007).

the tympanum. Taylor (1968, 57) believed the tympanum to be Anglo-Saxon but in a Norman fabric. For Pevsner (1975, 17) the tympanum belongs to the 'so-called Saxo-Norman overlap, i.e. quite probably to after 1066'. He recognized that the tympanum scrolls bore a striking similarity to early 11th-century illumination but observed that it is on Norman shafts (Pevsner 1975, 282). He considered that the tympanum, the capitals of the chancel arch and the single-splay chancel windows are Norman (Pevsner 1975, 282-283). Zarnecki (1978b, 183) argued against an Anglo-Saxon manuscript model for the tympanum and opted instead for a Norman source like an initial in a Jerome manuscript from Fécamp (Rouen, Bibl. Municipale, MS 445, fol. 72 recto) dated to *circa* 1100 by Alexander. He stated that 'the tympanum is not Anglo-Saxon as it has been claimed by several writers, but must date to the first decade of the twelfth century' (Zarnecki 1978b, 183). Cramp (2006, 240) included the tympanum in the section on 'Stones wrongly associated with pre-Conquest period'. She regarded the chancel-arch capitals as Romanesque and observed that in 1086 Knook was held by Leofgeat/Leofgyth who 'made and makes the King's and Queen's gold fringe' (Thorn & Thorn 1979, 67.86).

Fig. 11. Knook, chancel arch, S capital (© M. Thurlby, 2010).

Fig. 12. Knook, rear arch of nave S doorway (© M. Thurlby, 2007).

The manuscripts cited by Clapham and Zarnecki, although separated in date by about a hundred years, both appear visually convincing as parallels for the Knook tympanum. This is hardly surprising given the strong Anglo-Saxon influence on Norman illumination of the 11th and early 12th century (Kauffmann 1975, 19-20). Yet it is of little help in determining the date of the Knook tympanum. For this we have to consider the setting as a whole. Clapham is quite correct to relate the tympanum to the capitals of the south doorway and the chancel arch. The capitals of the south doorway are cushions with carved shields. The south capital of the chancel arch is also a cushion but here the foliage spreads over the entire capital (fig. 11), while on the north capital of the chancel arch the cushion shape is no longer defined in the foliage pattern. I have argued elsewhere (Thurlby 2003, 131-132; 2006, 43-44; cf. Harrison 1890; Gem 1987; Fernie 2000, 278-279) that cushion capitals were used in England before the Conquest, and in support of that I now add the cushion capital in Aelfric's Paraphrase of Pentateuch (B.L Cotton, Claudius B. IV, fol. 58 recto) (Dodwell and Clemoes 1974) of the second quarter of the 11th century. Be that as it may, while the foliage on the chancel arch capitals clearly belongs to the same family as that on the tympanum, its fleshier appearance tends to support a late 11th-century date. Something similar is encountered in the capitals of the north, south and west crossing arches at

Milborne Port where abaci are also omitted. The soffit roll of the south doorway may be related to both and Anglo-Saxon and a Norman tradition (Fernie 1983, 151, fig. 89; Fernie 2000, 274-276), but there are no pre-Conquest parallels for the attic bases which are similar to those at Tewkesbury abbey, *circa* 1090-1120 (Rigold 1977, 114-116, fig. 4, nos 61-62). Equally distinct post-Conquest Norman associations are seen in the constructional detail of the chancel north window – the other chancel windows are from Butterfield's 1876 restoration – and the form of the rear arch of the south doorway (fig. 12).

In the latter there are approximately equal sized radiating voussoirs, and there are neither through stones nor any large stones in the jambs. In other words, construction was not according to an Anglo-Saxon tradition but followed the new technology introduced from Romanesque Normandy (Gem 1988, 25). The evidence as a whole fits happily with attribution of Knook to Leofgeat around 1090. Her service as embroiderer to Edward the Confessor would account for the continuity of Anglo-Saxon motifs while her ongoing royal employment after the Conquest may explain the use of masons trained in the latest masonry techniques.

Egleton

Clapham (1933) regarded the south portal and chancel arch of St Edmund at Egleton (Rutland) as remarkable examples of the Saxo-Norman overlap and suggested that they were the only portions of the church 'immediately before or after the Conquest' (figs 13 and 14).

Against this, Cheetham opined that the south doorway, the chancel arch and a considerable portion of the nave south wall dated from the 12th century (Page 1935, 46). For the Taylors (1965, 228) the outer arch of the south doorway is of Norman character 'but it does not fit the curve of the tympanum and therefore seems to be a later addition'. A less-than- perfect fit between a tympanum and enclosing arch is not uncommon in Norman England and in the case of the Egleton south doorway is hardly sufficient reason to suggest that the tympanum predates the arch. Be that as it may, certain aspects of both the south doorway and the chancel arch speak clearly of Anglo-Saxon ancestry. The long tendrils with spiral terminations on the left capital of the south doorway and the capitals of the chancel arch may well derive from a pre-Conquest manuscript illumination like the borders of the Beatus Page of Cambridge, University Library, Ff. I. 23, fol. 5 (Temple 1976, cat 80, ill. 250). The huge, monolithic abaci recall examples like the imposts of the west doorway of Earls Barton tower, or in the arch to the south porticus at Breamore (Hampshire) where the stones have a cable border like the abaci of the Egleton south doorway. In these parallels the imposts sit atop squared jambs rather than jambs with bases, shafts and capitals as at Egleton. For this we may cite the north portal of St Botolph at Hadstock (Essex) (Fernie 2000, 214). The

Fig. 13. Egleton (Rutland), St Edmund, nave S doorway (© M. Thurlby, 2007).

Fig. 14. Egleton, chancel arch (© M. Thurlby, 2007).

disjunction between columns and arch mouldings in the Egleton south doorway is paralleled in the south doorway to the west tower at Broughton (Lincolnshire) and the chancel arch at Littleborough (Nottinghamshire) and Marton (Lincolnshire). Of these examples only Broughton may actually be pre-Conquest (Taylor & Taylor 1965, 115-116; Shapland 2008; cf. Brown 1925, 292), but the arrangement is quite unlike the logical

Norman placement of the support beneath the order of the arch. The other motifs at Egleton are most closely associated with Anglo-Norman work. The chevron in the arch of the south doorway frames double cones and thereby combines two motifs that are used separately on the blind arches and the window in the centre bay of the triforium on the exterior of the north transept at Norwich Cathedral (1096-1119). The nave clerestory at Norwich Cathedral has many cushion bases, plain versions of this motif on the left bases of the Egleton chancel arch (cf. Rigold 1977, 108). The Norwich bases are unlikely to pre-date 1110, and the same motif reappears in the vestibule to the great hall at Rising castle after 1138 (Thurlby 1996, 152). Aside from pre-Conquest manuscript parallels for the spiral-terminated tendrils on the Egleton capitals, the motif may also be associated with the south capitals of the arch to the west tower at St Mary at Tixover (Rutland) (Thurlby 2005, fig. 5). Similarly, the decorated shafts of the chancel arch and south doorway at Egleton belong to the same family as those on the west doorway at St Mary at Morcott (Rutland). Specifically, the lattice pattern on the south shaft of the chancel arch at Egleton is paralleled on the inner south shaft of the Morcott doorway (Thurlby 2005, fig 9), while the beading on the chevron on the north shaft of the chancel arch at Egleton relates to the beading on the cable on the north shaft at Morcott (Thurlby 2005, fig. 8). A case has been made for dating Tixover and Morcott to around 1130 (Thurlby 2005, 39-40), and the parallels cited give reason to believe that Egleton was built around the same time.

Kirkburn

Thomas Kendrick (1947, 120, pl. LXXXIV) discussed two Urnes style capitals at St Mary's, Kirkburn (Yorkshire) in the context of similar ornament on a panel at Jevington (Sussex) which he dated *circa* 1100. George Zarnecki (1951, 27-28, ills 17 and 18) followed this date but subsequently modified this view and dated the capitals with the church which he placed in the second half of the 12th century (Zarnecki 1966, 100 n.3). Baylé

Fig. 15. Kirkburn, (Yorks.), St Mary, N nave window 2, detail W capital (© M. Thurlby, 2010).

Fig. 16. Kirkburn, S nave, W window (© M. Thurlby, 2010).

(1991, 98, 103) opted for a late 11th or early 12th-century date for the Kirkburn capitals and referred to them in connection with a small group of sculptures at Sainte-Marie-du-Mont and Saint Côme-du-Mont (Manche). She subsequently suggested a date around 1120-1130 for Sainte-Marie-du-Mont (Baylé 1997, 105). She also associated two animals on the west capital in the second bay of the nave north wall at Kirkburn (fig. 15) with the pre-Conquest tradition and related sculpture at Autheuil (Orne) (Baylé 1991, 98, figs 310, 311 and 313).

The fabric of Kirkburn church is not dated by documentary evidence but the church was given to the Augustinian priory of Guisborough by its founder Robert de Brus II (d. 1141) probably in 1119 and certainly before 1124 (Brown 1889, vi-x, 3). Pevsner (1972, 295-296) dated Kirkburn about twenty years after the foundation. The Urnes-style capitals in question are not easily dated with reference to their architectural setting in the westernmost window on the south side of the four-bay aisleless nave (fig. 16).

Here they carry the roll moulding of a slightly pointed arch which encloses trefoil plate tracery above two pointed lights. The window in bay two of the nave south wall and the windows in the nave north wall have traditional Romanesque round arches carved with chevron on carved capitals. This suggests that the plate tracery window was the product of a remodelling in the late 12th or 13th century. In contrast to this, the capital with animal sculpture is part of round-headed window with chevron in the arch which is undoubtedly part of the original fabric (fig. 15). Crucial for the dating of the Kirkburn capitals is the three-order south doorway which is adorned with elaborately decorated point-to-point chevrons on order two, and beakhead on order three (fig. 17).

The chevron is far removed from typologically 'early' types but what this means in terms of absolute dating is not easily determined. Chevron is notoriously difficult to date precisely and it is important to bear in mind that

Fig. 17. Kirkburn, S doorway (© M. Thurlby, 2010).

chevron with foliated lozenges in the soffit is used in the outer arch of the north portal at Cormac's Chapel, Cashel (Co. Tipperary) before 1134 (Moss 2009). More precise for the date of the Kirkburn portal is the inclusion of beakhead which first appears in the 1120s at Sarum Cathedral and Reading abbey (Henry and Zarnecki 1957-8; Zarnecki, Holt & Holland 1984, 174; Fernie 2000, 277; Baxter and Harrison 2002; Thurlby 2008). Beakhead ornament was to enjoy great popularity in Yorkshire but none of the examples is precisely dated. Reading abbey was the work of King Henry I, and Sarum Cathedral was built for Bishop Roger (1102-1139) who was second only in importance to the king. It is likely that ambitious patrons of architecture would wish to emulate such works without delay. Kirkburn is indeed the product of an ambitious patron for quite apart from the rich decoration of the fabric it is constructed throughout in fine ashlar, a mark of rare distinction in a parish church and one that

Fig. 18. Kirkstall abbey (Yorks), nave W window, detail of label stop (© M. Thurlby, 2010).

groups it with great cathedral and abbey churches. It is tempting to attribute construction to Robert de Brus II in the late 1120s after the gift of the church to Guisborough priory. If this attribution is correct then it is interesting that a patron of Norman descent should have incorporated pre-Conquest motifs in the decoration of his church. When seen in the context of Maylis Baylé's associations with similar sculpture in Normandy, there can be no doubt that Anglo-Saxon motifs had been fully assimilated into Norman taste.

Late 12th and 13th century

References to Anglo-Saxon exemplars continued into the second half of the 12th century and the early 13th century. At Kirkstall abbey, commenced in 1152, the Anglo-Saxon character of the interlace is evident on certain capitals, bases, a corbel and a piscina (Irvine 1892; Thurlby 1995a, 66) and the former east rose window (Harrison 1995). The pattern of the latter may be compared with the south belfry window of the west tower at Barnack (Taylor and Taylor 1965, fig. 22). In addition, the hood moulds of the nave west windows (Hope 1907, 22) terminate in heads of muzzled bears (fig. 18), like pre-Conquest hogback tombs as at Brompton-in-Allerton (Yorkshire).

At Malmesbury abbey, Kit Galbraith (1965) demonstrated the importance of Anglo-Saxon iconographic sources for the sculpture on the arch to the south porch. The heads of the angels above apostles in the side lunettes of the south porch take on a distinctly Anglo-Saxon profile. The iconography of the early gospel cycle on the north doorway of the Lady Chapel at Glastonbury abbey also reveals Anglo-Saxon iconographic sources (Thurlby 1995b, 138-140). At Wells Cathedral we witness precise Anglo-Saxon references in the retrospective effigies of bishops (Reeve 1998), and in the stiff-leaf capitals (Gardner 1927, 4, 22-26; Wynn-Reeves 1952). For various aspects of the west front, such as quatrefoils and trefoil niches, Paul Binski (2004, 109, 117-118) cited Anglo-Saxon associations which extend to the Chorus of Virgins in the Benedictional of St Ethelwold (London, British Library Add. MS 49598). To these we might add the canopy over the Coronation of the Virgin with the sharply pointed gable integrated into the trefoil arch in relation to the enclosing arches in the evangelist portraits in the mid-eleventh-century gospels in Monte Cassino (Archivio della Badia, MS BB. 437, 439), in which there are also proto stiff-leaf capitals (Temple 1976, cat. 95, ills 287 and 288).

Conclusion

The Anglo-Saxon tradition in architectural sculpture and articulation after the Conquest has been experienced in a number of ways. At Bibury and Langford the continuity of Anglo-Saxon forms is witnessed virtually without change. At Milborne Port aspects of Anglo-Saxon continuity are juxtaposed with new elements not least with regard to Norman masonry technique. Knook provides something similar but in contrast to this there is evidence at Egleton for the longevity of Anglo-Saxon masonry technique into the first third of the 12th century. At this time Kirkburn illustrates the appeal of Anglo-Saxon motifs to a Norman patron in an otherwise entirely Norman building. This tradition is continued in aspects of Kirkstall abbey. Anglo-Saxon references at Malmesbury abbey may have been inspired through reverence for St Aldhelm while at Glastonbury abbey such associations speak of the proud pre-Conquest history of the site. Similar considerations were at work at Wells not least to draw attention to its place as the historical seat of the see before it had been usurped by Bath.

Acknowledgements

I am grateful to Richard Bryant, Eric Fernie and Stuart Harrison for answering questions in connection with this paper.

Bibliography

Bagshaw, S., Bryant, R. and Hare, M. 2006. 'The Discovery of an Anglo-Saxon Painted Figure at St Mary's Church, Deerhurst, Gloucestershire', *Antiquaries Journal*, 86, 66-109

Barker, P. 1994. *A Short Architectural History of Worcester Cathedral*, Worcester Cathedral Publications: 2 (Worcester)

Barral i Altet, X. 1989. *Belgique romane*, Zodiaque (La Pierre-qui-Vire, Yonne)

Batcock, N. 1988. 'The Parish Church in Norfolk in the 11th and 12th Centuries', in Blair 1988, 179-190

Baxter, R & Harrison, S. 2002. 'The Decoration of the Cloister at Reading Abbey' in *Windsor: Medieval Archaeology, Art and Architecture of the Thames Valley: The British Archaeological Association Conference Transactions*, XXV, ed. L. Keen and E. Scarff , W.S. Maney and Son Ltd (Leeds), 302-12.

Baylé, M. 1980. Ancienne abbatiale Notre-Dame de Bernay', *Congrès archéologique*, 138: 119-162

Baylé, M. 1991. *Les origines et les premiers developpements de la sculpture romane en Normadie: Art de Basse-Normandie*, No. 100 (Caen)

Baylé, M 1992. 'Frises et dalles sculptées dans l'architecture romane de Normandie', in D. Kahn (ed.), *The Romanesque Frieze and its Spectator*, Harvey Miller Publishers (London): 75-83

Baylé, M. 1997. 'Sainte-Marie-du-Mont: église Notre-Dame', in M. Baylé (ed.), L'architecture normande au moyen age', 2 vols, Presses Universitaires de Caen/Éditions Chales Corlet (Caen/Condé-sur-Noireau), 2: 105-107

Binski, P, 2004. *Becket's Crown: Art and Imagination in Gothic England 1170-1300*, Yale University Press (New Haven and London)

Bird, W.H. 1928. *Old Gloucestershire churches: a concise guide, especially compiled for motoring folk and others interested in the architecture of our churches, and also their contents, screens, fonts, brasses, etc.*, Ed. J. Burrow and Co Ltd (London and Cheltenham)

Blair, J. 1985. 'Secular Minster Churches in Domesday Book', in P. Sawyer (ed.), *Domesday Book: a Reassessment*, E. Arnold (London): 104-142

Blair, J. (ed.) 1988. *Minsters and Parish Churches: The Local Church in Transition 950-1200*, Oxford University Committee for Archaeology (Oxford)

Blair, John, 1994. *Anglo-Saxon Oxfordshire*, Alan Sutton Publishing Ltd (Stroud)

Brooks, N. 2005. 'Introduction: how do we know about St Wulfstan', in J. Brown and N.P. Brooks (eds), *St Wulfstan and His World*, Ashgate (Aldershot): 151-166

Brown, G.B. 1925. *The Arts in Early England, Anglo-Saxon Architecture*, John Murray (London)

Brown, W (ed.). 1889. *Cartularium prioratus de Gyseburne*, Publications of the Surtees Society, LXXXVI

Cambridge, E. 1994. ' Early Romanesque Architecture in North-East England: A Style and its Patrons', in D. Rollason, M. Harvey & M. Prestwich, *Anglo-Norman Durham 1093-1193*, Boydell and Brewer (Woodbridge): 141-160

Clapham, A.W. 1930. *English Romanesque Architecture before the Conquest*, Clarendon Press (Oxford)

Clapham, A.W. 1933. 'Egleton Church', *Archaeological Journal*, 90, 399 and pl. XIX

Clapham, A.W. 1934. *English Romanesque Architecture after the Conquest*, Clarendon Press (Oxford)

Clapham, A.W. 1947. 'Knook Church', *Archaeological Journal*, 104: 163

Cramp, R. 2006. *Corpus of Anglo-Saxon Sculpture, VII, South-West England*, The British Academy by Oxford University Press (Oxford)

Croome, W.J. 1953. 'Gloucestershire Churches', *Transactions of the Bristol and Gloucestershire Archaeological Society*, 72: 5-22

Currie, C.R.J (ed). 1999. *VCH Somerset*, VII, Oxford University Press (Oxford)

Darlington, R.R (ed.). 1928. *The Vita Wulfstani of William of Malmesbury*, Royal Historical Society (London)

Dodwell C.R. and Clemoes, P (ed.) 1974. *The Old English Illustrated Pentateuch: British Museum Cotton Claudius B. IV*, Rosenkilde og Bagger (Copenhagen)

Fernie, E.C. 1977. 'The Romanesque Piers of Norwich Cathedral', *Norfolk Archaeology*, 36: 383-386

Fernie, E.C. 1983. *The Architecture of the Anglo-Saxon*, B.T. Batsford (London)

Fernie, E.C. 2000. *The Architecture of Norman England*, Oxford University Press (Oxford)

Foster, S. 1987. 'A Gazetteer of the Anglo-Saxon Sculpture in Historic Somerset', *Somerset Archaeology and Natural History*, 131: 49-80

Galbraith, K.J. 1965. 'The Iconography of the Biblical Scenes at Malmesbury Abbey', *Journal of the British Archaeological Association*, series 3, 28: 39-56

Gardner, S. 1927. *English Gothic Foliage Sculpture*, Cambridge University Press (Cambridge)

Gem, R. 1984. 'L'architecture préromane et romane en Angleterre: problèmes d'origine et de chronologie', *Bulletin Monumental*, 147: 233-272

Gem, R. 1986. 'The Bishop's Chapel at Hereford: The Roles of Patron and Craftsman', in Sarah Macready and F.H. Thompson (eds), *Art and Patronage in the English Romanesque*, Society of Antiquaries of London Occasional Paper (New Series) VIII: 87-96

Gem, R. 1987. 'Canterbury and the Cushion Capital', a Commentary on Passages from Goscelin's "*De Miraculis Sancti Augustini*" in N. Stratford (ed.), *Romanesque and Gothic: Essays for George Zarnecki*, Boydell Press (Woodbridge): 83-105

Gem, R. 1988. 'The English Parish Church in the 11th and early 12th Centuries', in Blair 1988: 21-30

Gem, R. & Howe, E., with contributions from Richard Bryant. 2008. 'The Ninth-Century Polychrome Decoration at St Mary's Church, Deerhurst, *Antiquaries Journal*, 88: 109-164

Gem, R. & Tudor-Craig, P. 1981. 'A "Winchester School" Painting at Nether Wallop, Hampshire', *Anglo-Saxon England*, 9: 115-136

Harrison, J. P. 1890. 'Anglo-Norman Ornament compared with Designs in Anglo-Saxon MSS', *Archaeological Journal*, 47: 142-153

Harrison, S.A. 1995. 'Kirkstall Abbey: The 12th-Century Window Tracery and Rose Window', *Yorkshire Monasticism: Archaeology, Art and Architecture: British Archaeological Association Conference Transactions*, XVI, ed. L.R. Hoey: 73-78

Heighway, C. 1987. *Anglo-Saxon Gloucestershire*, Alan Sutton and Gloucestershire County Library (Gloucester)

Henry, F. and Zarnecki, G. 1957-1958. 'Romanesque Arches Decorated with Human and Animal Heads', *Journal of the British Archaeological Association*, 3rd ser., 20-21: 1-35

Hope, W.H St John and Bilson, J. 1907 'Architectural Description of Kirkstall Abbey', *The Publications of the Thoresby Society*, XVI: 1-140

Irvine, J.T. 1892. 'Notes on Specimens of Interlacing Ornament at Kirkstall Abbey' *Journal of the British Archaeological Association*, XLVIII: 26-30

Kauffmann, C.M. 1975. *A Survey of Manuscripts Illuminated in the British Isles, III, Romanesque Manuscripts 1066-1190*, Harvey Miller Publishers (London)

Kendrick, T.D. 1949. *Late Saxon and Viking Art*, Methuen (London)

Keynes, S. 1987. 'Regembald the Chancellor', *Anglo-Norman Studies*, 10: 185-222

Keyser, C.E. 1918-19. 'Visit to the Churches of Barnsley, Bibury, Aldsworth, Winson, Coln Rogers, and Coln St Denys', *Ttransactions of the Bristol and Gloucestershire Archaeological Society*, 41: 171-204

Moore, J.S. 1982. *Domesday Book, Gloucestershire*, Phillimore (Chichester)

Morris, J. 1978. *Domesday Book, Oxfordshire*, Phillimore (Chichester)

Moss, R. 2009. *Romanesque Chevron Ornament: The language of British, Norman and Irish sculpture in the twelfth century*, BAR International Series 1908 (Oxford)

Page W (ed.) 1935. *VCH Rutland*, II, Archibald Constable and Company Limited (London)

Pevsner, N. 1958. *The Buildings of England, South and West Somerset*, Penguin Books (Harmondsworth)

Pevsner, N. 1972. *The Buildings of England, Yorkshire: York and The East Riding*, Penguin Books (Harmondsworth)

Pevsner, N. 1975. *The Buildings of England, Wiltshire*, 2nd edn rev. by B. Cherry, Penguin Books (Harmondsworth)

RCHME 1924. Royal Commission on Historical Monuments (England): *An Inventory of the Historical Monuments in London, I, Westminster Abbey*, H.M.S.O. (London)

Reeve, M.M. 1998. 'The Retrospective Effigies of Anglo-Saxon Bishops at Wells Cathedral', *Somerset Archaeology and Natural History*, 142: 235-59

Rigold, S.E. 1977. 'Romanesque Bases, in and South-east of the limestone belt', in M.R. Apted, R. Gilyard-Beer and A.D. Saunders,*Ancient Monuments and Their Interpretation: Essays Presented to A.J. Taylor*, Phillmore (Chichester): 99-137

Shapland, M. 2008. 'St Mary's, Broughton, Lincolnshire: A Thegnly Tower-Nave in the Late Anglo-Saxon Landscape', *Archaeological Journal*, 165: 471-519

Stocker, D. & Everson, P. 2006. *Summoning St Michael: Early Romanesque Towers in Lincolnshire*, Oxbow Books (Oxford)

Taylor, H.M. and Taylor, J. 1965. *Anglo-Saxon Architecture*, 2 vols, Cambridge University Press (Cambridge)

Taylor, H.M. and Taylor, J. 1966. 'Architectural Sculpture in Pre-Norman England', *Journal of the British Archaeological Association*, 3rd ser., 29: 3-51

Taylor, H.M. 1968, 'Anglo-Saxon Sculpture at Knook', *Wiltshire Archaeological and Natural History Magazine*, 63: 54-57

Temple, E. 1976. *A Survey of Manuscripts Illuminated in the British Isles, II, Anglo-Saxon Manuscripts 900-1066*, Harvey Miller Publishers (London)

Thorn, C. and Thorn, F. 1979. *Domesday Book, Wiltshire*, Phillimore (Chichester)

Thorn, C. and Thorn, F. 1980. *Domesday Book, Somerset* Phillimore (Chichester)

Thurlby, M, 1994. 'The Roles of the Patron and the Master Mason in the First Design of Durham Cathedral', in D. Rollason, M. Harvey & M. Prestwich (eds), *Anglo-Norman Durham 1093-1193*, Boydell and Brewer (Woodbridge): 161-184

Thurlby, M. 1995a. 'Some Design Aspects of Kirkstall Abbey', in *Yorkshire Monasticism: Archaeology, Art and Architecture: British Archaeological Association Conference Transactions*, XVI, ed. L. R. Hoey: 62-72

Thurlby, M. 1995b. 'The Lady Chapel of Glastonbury Abbey', *Antiquaries Journal*, 65 (1995): 107-170

Thurlby, M. 1996. 'The Influence of Norwich Cathedral on Romanesque Architecture in East Anglia', in *Norwich Cathedral: Church, City and Diocese 1096-1996*, ed. Ian Atherton, Eric Fernie, Christopher Harper-Bill and Hassell Smith (London and Rio Grande: The Hambledon Press, 1996): 136-157

Thurlby, M, 1999. *The Herefordshire School of Romanesque Sculpture*, Logaston Press (Almeley [Herefs.])

Thurlby, M, 2003a. 'Anglo-Saxon Architecture Beyond the Millennium: Its Continuity in Norman Building', in N. Hiscock (ed.), *The White Mantle of Churches: Architecture, Liturgy and Art Around the Millennium*, Brepols (Turnhout, Belgium): 119-137

Thurlby, M. 2005. 'The Romanesque Churches of St Mary Magdalen at Tixover and St Mary at Morcott', *Ecclesiology Today*, 35: 23-41 http://www.ecclsoc.org/ET.35.pdf

Thurlby, M. 2006. *Romanesque Architecture and Sculpture in Wales* (Logaston)

Thurlby, M. 2008. 'Sarum Cathedral as rebuilt by Roger, Bishop of Salisbury, 1102-1139: the state of research and open questions', *Wiltshire Archaeological and Natural History Magazine*, 101: 130-140

Tweddle, D., Biddle, M & Kjølbye-Biddle, B. 1995. *Corpus of Anglo-Saxon Sculpture, IV, South-East England*, The British Academy by Oxford University Press (Oxford)

Tudor-Craig, P. 1990. 'Nether Wallop Reconsidered', in S. Cather, D. Park, and P. Williamson (eds), *Early Medieval Wall Painting and Painted Sculpture in England*, BAR British Series, 216: 89-104

Verey, D. and Brooks, A. 2002. *The Buildings of England, Gloucestershire 1: The Cotswolds*, Yale University Press (New Haven and London)

Wynn-Reeves, P. 1952. 'English Stiff-Leaf Sculpture', unpublished PhD thesis, University of London

Zarnecki, G. 1951. *English Romanesque Sculpture 1066-1140*, Alec Trianti (London)

Zarnecki, G. 1955. 'Winchester Acanthus in Romanesque Sculpture', *Wallraf Richatrz Jahrbuch*, 17: 211-215; reprinted in Zarnecki 1979

Zarnecki, G. 1958. *The Early Sculpture of Ely Cathedral*, Alec Tiranti (London)

Zarnecki, G. 1966. '1066 and Architectural Sculpture', *Proceedings of the British Academy*, 52: 87-104; reprinted in Zarnecki 1979

Zarnecki, G. 1978a. 'The Romanesque Capitals in the South Transept of Worcester Cathedral', *Medieval Art and Architecture at Worcester Cathedral: British Archaeological Association Conference Transactions*, ed. G. Popper, W.S. Maney and Sons Ltd (Leeds): 38-42

Zarnecki, G. 1978b. 'Romanesque Sculpture in Normandy and England in the Eleventh Century', *Proceedings of the Battle Conference on Anglo-Norman Studies, 1*: 168-189, 233-235.

Zarnecki, G. 1979. *Studies in Romanesque Sculpture*, The Dorian Press (London)

Zarnecki, G; Holt, J. & Holland, T (eds) 1984. *English Romanesque Art 1066-1200*, Hayward Gallery London, 5 April – 8 July 1984, Arts Council of Great Britain in association with Weidenfeld and Nicholson (London)

Laser Scanning of the Inscribed Hiberno-Romanesque Arch at Monaincha, Co. Tipperary, Ireland

Orla Murphy, Ph.D., University College, Cork

The primary function of any preservation or conservation measure is to record immediately the monument or site under threat. Historically this has been achieved by using technologies that were limited to two-dimensional representation including photographic records, drawings, and rubbings. However, small-scale models and replica casts have also been utilised to record heritage data.

The outcomes generated by using laser-scanning technology, a three-dimensional tool, offer the possibility of replica creation and a manoeuvrable digital image that may be used in a variety of ways. This three- dimensional dataset is malleable enough to support conservation, preservation and education efforts. Laser- scanning has sub-millimetre accuracy and can create a permanent three-dimensional record of objects now recognized to be impermanent. It is achieved through the use of the laser and triangulating data points.

The Polhemus FastSCAN handheld laser scanner is a non-contact digitiser that allows for the fast scanning of three-dimensional objects. This non-contact element is a vital aspect of the process as it ensures that the object scanned is unharmed by the methodology whereas rubbings or making casts have the potential to damage a fragile artefact.

The scanning process is much like spray-painting the object with light: a laser-beam emitted by a wand is smoothly swept over the object. A main component of the system is a processing unit, about the size of a desktop computer, which takes care of the registration process in real time in order to combine together the overlapping sweeps. The wand itself is a non-contact range finder, based on the simultaneous projection and detection of laser-light (using plane of light technology) coupled with a magnetic system to keep track of the position and orientation of the wand.

When activated, this wand emits a laser-beam (a Class II laser, 1mW at a wavelength of 670nm) that is read by one of two cameras mounted on each end, while the 3D location of the profile is computed by triangulation using the magnetic tracking system. The processing unit plugs into the computer's printer port, and the wand connects into this unit.

The software is RapidForm2004 Origin from INUS Technology Inc.—a powerful reverse engineering software that enables the construction of a complete 3D digital model from a point cloud. This software is a leading application used in a wide variety of technical fields, including mass-customisation, graphics animation, rapid inspection, and 3D photography to create 3D digital models.

The use of two-dimensional digital imaging to enhance manuscript quality and legibility has been an acknowledged technique for years, using drawing, measurement and photography. It was a logical progression to look at ways of representing monuments in three dimensions, and also to explore methods of enhancing decayed inscriptions.

The team begins with a real object and generates a 3D model. In one case we scanned a very early high cross shaft that had been inscribed. What initially seems to be a continuous surface on the model is a set of linked points in space, like pixels in a digital image. In the initial image of the positive cast of the Toureen Peacaun inscription model in our sample, the inscribed area is 37.4 cm x 73.4 cm in height consisting of 411,000 vertices and 821,000 triangles in the model (Murphy *et al* 2007).

When the image is thus captured, it is possible to adjust the ambient, diffuse and specular colours of the material, as well as a shininess parameter, in order to enhance the legibility of the characters of the inscription. The resulting 3D file can be lit from various directions, its surface texture can be changed and its relief can be exaggerated.

One of the possibilities of the software process is called minimum curvature texturing. In this case, the computer searches for the flattest curve that will pass through a given point on the surface. If the point is at the bottom of a depression – like an inscribed letter – then it has a negative value. The computer collates numbers for each point. Then, in order to make the numbers visible, the negative values are assigned a particular, perhaps darker, colour. This, then, is not at all like a normal photograph: it is a mapping of numerical values that record curvature.

If there is a low frequency in height across the model (for example a shallow dip, top to bottom, like a valley) this impedes a clear reading of the inscription. In order to remove it, the image is processed again using wavelet filtering.

Fig. 1. First use of the laser scanner in the field (© O. Murphy, 2007).

Fig. 2. Scan of positive cast, inscribed cross-shaft at Toureen Peacaun (© O. Murphy, 2007).

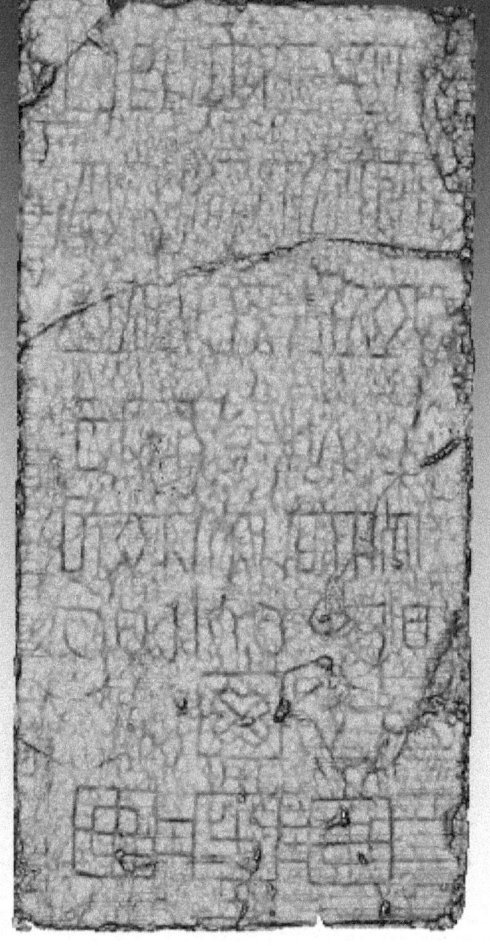

Fig. 3. Minimum curvature texturing, inscribed cross-shaft at Toureen Peacaun (© O. Murphy, 2007).

Fig. 4. Hiberno-Romanesque arch at Monaincha (© O. Murphy, 2007).

It is also possible to make movies from the 3D model. A synthetic video sequence is generated by importing the 3D model into 3D Studio Max software. An artificial texture with high reflectance properties is applied to the model, and different light conditions are stimulated by moving the artificial projected light source around it.

The results greatly enhance the viewer's appreciation of the object, and contribute to conservation, preservation, education and research efforts.

Scanning at Monaincha, Co. Tipperary

The ruined remains of the church at Monaincha, Co. Tipperary, have been recorded as a place of retreat since the seventh century. It has been associated with saints Canice of Aghaboe and also Crónán of Roscrea. There is also a reference in the *Annals of Ulster* for the year 806 that reads: 'Elarius, ancorita 7 scriba Locha Cre, dormiuit' ('In this year Elarius, anchorite and scribe of Loch Cré fell asleep'). Monaincha was once one of two islands in a bog, which is now drained. Of the two islands only one remains.

Today, Monaincha is an arresting site. The enclosure as it now stands is elevated and striking. It is marked on its southwestern edge by two huge beech trees, which lean away from the remaining structure. The site is well-kept and far from traffic. The enclosure is at the east of the original settlement and comprises a low stone wall that marks out the twelfth-century church and its later addition of a sacristy. There is a twelfth-century high cross at the western end of the site. This is situated just beyond the doorway in the west gable which is framed by the focus of this paper, the inscribed Hiberno-Romanesque arch.

Although it is very scenic, these factors also meant that this monument posed challenges for data-capture. As at Toureen Peacaun, this monument is in situ in the open air. The twelfth-century church is now situated on an elevated, exposed site in the middle of a large field. On one occasion we scanned through a hailstorm. The scanner proved itself weather-proof at Monaincha. It scanned in wet, cold, damp and frosty conditions. It is lightweight, portable and only requires two people to operate it. No heavy generator is necessary; for power we used two twelve-volt car batteries.

Previously scholars have debated whether the inscription read:

'OR DO C', 'OR DO T', or 'OR DO C ... S'.

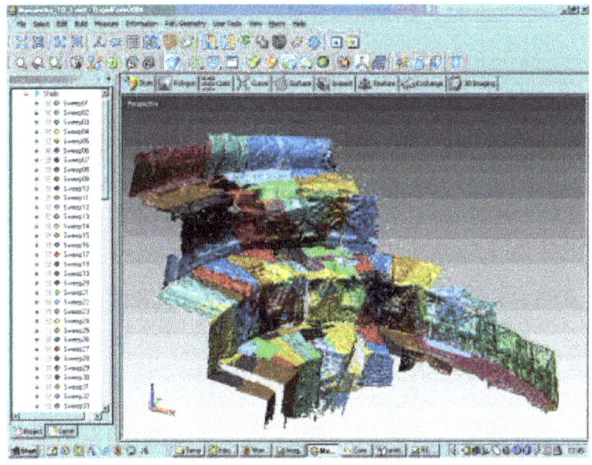

Fig. 5. Rapidform sweeps of one section of arch (© O. Murphy, 2007).

The decision to scan the inscribed Hiberno-Romanesque arch at Monaincha in Co. Tipperary was the most ambitious test of the hand-held scanner undertaken by the project. The scale of the monument, its situation, and the three-dimensional nature of the sculpture in relief within the arch, all combined to make this the most challenging of the inscribed stones for all aspects of the technology.

If we had simply scanned the inscription on the pilaster of the southern jamb of the arch, the model would have been complete within twenty-four hours. However, the decision was taken to scan the decorated orders of the arch in their entirety, with their outer pilasters, and this meant that the scanning took four days and four separate visits to complete.

Fig. 6. Partially-modelled image, contrasting standard photography with digital technology (© O. Murphy, 2007).

Fig. 7. Inscription photographed in situ (© O. Murphy, 2007).

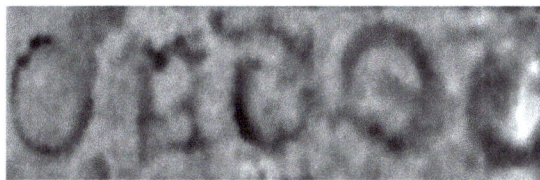

Fig. 8. Scanned and modelled inscription in grayscale (© O. Murphy, 2007).

Fig. 9. Scanned and modelled inscription in green with high-reflectance properties (© O. Murphy, 2007).

The second arch-ring proved most intricate and complex. It is difficult to reach, as it is between the first and third rings, and the decoration of chevron and roll moulding outlined with pellets was extremely difficult to scan from all angles in order to perfect the model. Unlike the scanning of a two-dimensional image, the laser-light had to reach the back of the mouldings, which was a difficult task given the structure of the arch itself. Fig. 5 shows the amount of registered sweeps generated in order to attempt a model. This image reflects only the registered sweeps; many more sweeps were attempted before these were finally chosen.

Unlike an inscription, the decorative elements within the orders of the arch are almost identical and repetitive. Chevrons visualised through the malleable three dimensions of the software look very alike. Due to the need for speed and accuracy in processing the large file sizes, my colleague, Dr. Thierry Daubos, from the Department of Experimental Physics, NUIG, elected to perform numerous smaller scans of the surface area, creating a patchwork using smaller sweeps. The repeating pattern made this very time consuming. On one occasion, a section of the arch was missed, necessitating a return trip to scan again.

To conclude, the resulting image of the arch with its inscription on the southern pilaster is an example of what may be achieved with this laser scanner. The data-capture was achieved in all weather conditions, far from mains power sources. It is a complete digital replica of the arch in situ, from which a model of any size may be generated with sub-millimetre accuracy.

The scale of the arch at Monaincha presented the greatest challenge for the technology. The inscription on the south side of the arch is short, and we were able to contribute to existing scholarship, and stating, confidently, that letter-forms previously legible further down the pilaster are now gone, and that the letter previously thought to be 'C' may be read as 'T'. It was notable that even in such a remote location, monuments were subjected to damage.

We succeeded in generating a digital model of the arch which allows viewers in digital environments to progress from a frontal view to a detail of the inner arch face, revealing a close-up of the inscription. This constitutes a significant improvement on traditional two-dimensional representation. The software can also generate line-drawings, and monochrome images of any aspect of the model. This further increases the accessibility and functionality of digital models.

The digitized data, in this case the models, are such that they may be presented in many forms: two-dimensional, three-dimensional, hard-copy, electronic and virtual. Thus, they can be accessed by many levels of viewer / interrogator; they may be enjoyed simply for their aesthetic quality, or in the spirit of this paper, promote a meaningful way for all levels of interested stakeholders to access and participate in this interdisciplinary approach.

Acknowledgements

This project was part of the PRTLI-funded 'Foundations of Irish Culture' project at the National University of Ireland, Galway, funded by the Higher Education Authority under the National Development Plan.

Bibliography

Murphy O. *et al*, 2007. "A Virtual Archive of Inscribed Stones", in J. Elkins (ed.), *In Visual Practices Across the University*. Wilhelm Fink Verlag (München): 215 – 222

www.ingramcontent.com/pod-product-compliance
Lightning Source LLC
Chambersburg PA
CBHW061549010526
44115CB00023B/2994